Over The Top

(From Under-the-Bridge)

Short Biographies of Ten Remarkable Men

by

Frank Mason

FOREWORD

I count it a privilege to commend Frank Mason's studies of a dozen remarkable men, in *Over The Top.* His title reminds us that there are heroes of peace, as well as of war. "Foreheads of men have bled, where no wounds were". The men Mr Mason describes have been outstanding in their professional lives and in service to the community. Some, like Jack Jones, C.H., founder of ACAS and sometime leader of the Transport and General Worker's Union, are already famous. Others would have remained unsung heroes, but for Frank Mason's informed and sympathetic account of their achievements.

What is perhaps even more astonishing than their individual attainments, is the fact that they had their roots in "the little chapel" — Banks Road Wesleyan Methodist Chapel, Garston, Liverpool. They grew up in a tough, working-class area, and often had a hard struggle to find proper scope for their gifts. The Scout Troop at Banks Road was formative for them. They were shaped in that troop by devoted leaders, whose service was rooted in their commitment to Christ and the Church. The sacrificial work of such leaders, including Frank himself, produced a marvellous harvest of character and service. Dan Oakes, a blacksmith, became a minister of the Australian Methodist Church, gave pioneer missionary service in New Guinea, and died in Japanese hands in 1942. Dr. David Goodall served for thirteen years as a medical missionary in India, and is today a distinguished gynaecologist. Keith Goodall has risen to be Chief Ambulance Officer for South Glamorgan, and at 38 was the youngest-ever President of the Association of Chief Ambulance Officers.

It is men of this calibre of whom Frank Mason writes, in an eminently readable style. Increasingly we recognize that "Small is beautiful". It certainly was — and is — at the little chapel in Banks Road. Behind all these stories of superb personal achievement, there stands a loving, praying, caring fellowship, who were faithful to Christ's call to "Feed my sheep" and "tend my lambs". That fellowship produced Frank Mason himself. In writing this impressive book, he has not only repaid something of what he owes to Banks Road; he has put every one who reads it in his debt.

JOHN A NEWTON
Chairman of the Liverpool District of the Methodist Church; Moderator of the Free Church Federal Council, 1989/90.

CONTENTS

First published 1990 by Countyvise Limited, 1 & 3 Grove Road, Rock Ferry, Birkenhead, Wirral, Merseyside L42 3XS.

Photoset and printed by Birkenhead Press Limited, 1 & 3 Grove Road, Rock Ferry, Birkenhead, Merseyside L42 3XS.

ISBN 0 907768 37 7.

INTRODUCTION

The horrific trench-warfare of the 1914-18 war gave vital significance to the bravery and uncertainty of young soldiers who leapt from the comparative safety of their trench and stumbled through the cannon barrage of "no-mans-land". Tragically, thousands perished.

My anthology of the gallantry of *civilian heroes* who went "over the top" in their youth, distinguishing themselves by their achievements for mankind in general, thankfully recognizes their "guts" and wisdom. All gave themselves in ideals nurtured in a little chapel in a little region of a small suburb of Liverpool, within a few years of the termination of the carnage of that first Great World War.

Only one of my heroes was called to lay down his life; he became a christian martyr in British New Guinea in 1942. One, still living, was declared by a B.B.C. gallop poll in the 1970's to be the "most powerful man in Britain". One other became a naval chaplain, decorated with the O.B.E., but most of them just pursued their civilian life with a zest and happy spirit which bounced them to notoriety.

Let me tell you about the *"little chapel!"*

In the mid-1840's GARSTON was an insignificant village on the River Mersey $5^1/_2$ miles south of the growing port of Liverpool. Gradually evolving from rural and fishing dependancy by the introduction of industrial works and docks, workers' dwellings multiplied and a few christians started a Sunday School in dockside premises. By the 1870's a little Wesleyan Chapel had been built, succeeded by *"our little chapel",* opened in 1883.

The writer began to attend that chapel and Sunday School just before his fifth birthday. I remember it well-error-with horror! My two elder brothers relunctantly took me, thrust me into the empty schoolroom, and left me. The vast hall and remote high ceiling frightened me so I dived under a substantial wooden form and remained, crouched, until forcibly extricated. Nothing else of that day clings to my memory, but later there were more interesting things to recollect. Abutting the school-room was a large alcove with ascending steps to give crowded seating to about eighty little primary bottoms. The little ones within the alcove could witness the opening exercises of the junior department until tall folding doors could draw a veil over the efforts of two young ladies to achieve two things — one, reasonable silence and two, the telling of bible stories. Their success rate seemed to be about three-to-one in reverse.

The 'little chapel' 1883-1970 with the New Schoolroom 1927, in the foreground.

A wedding in the 'little chapel'

Wedged on our hard seats, a captive audience, we were graduated up the five ascending rows according to seniority. Older and more brash, the back row boys discovered that they could slide down on the rounded head of the wooden containing wall, causing not only consternation to the teachers but painful consequences to the little ones over whom the culprits had to climb back to their exalted positions. When we rose to junior scholar status, the schoolroom, containing over a hundred children, looked less forbidding than at my first introduction; moreover one could look to the right and see those little kids in the gallery alcove. More soberly, we knew that on the left, behind two polished doors leading into the chapel, were about 150 big lads and girls, the seniors.

Looking back in time, one could have been in sympathy with that gospel character, *Nathanael* who, when *Philip* invited him to come and see *Jesus,* said: "Can anything *good* come out of *Nazareth*?" *Could* anything good come out of the motley 350 disadvantaged children whose parents, unemployed or working slavish hours, were lowly and angry? But always there was "disadvantaged" adults and teenagers who would give time and enthusiasm to teach, run youth groups and guilds, getting joy as they served one another, and enjoying each other's company.

Whence the term *"Under-the-Bridge"*?

As the Mersey riverside developed and the Lancashire coal fields offered fuel to distant ports, railway lines and docks became an answer. Only one roadway served as entrance to the growing community adjacent to the new docks and works, so a railway bridge had to span that life-line and "Under-the-Bridge" remained a secluded community. Down river, towards Liverpool, a railway network to the docks contrasted with the woods and farmland enclosing the other end of the estate. Fostering their own shops and schools, the community had little need to pass the bridge boudary until later years when wider amenities, library, swimming baths and cinema entertainments, thrived in the "better parts of Garston".

Overcrowding then started emigrations but of the thousand or more dwellings some streets had up to 50% homes with some connection with the "little chapel". The Parish Church, just at the entrance to the area, sustained a day-school and later a Roman Catholic church and school were built.

The parents of one boy favoured the Parish Church and he sang in their church choir, but he was educated at the council school next to the Wesleyan chapel — one could throw a stone to either place from his*Stanley Street* home. This circumstance caused him to have a special place in this book and in the chapel that reared many distinctive men and women.

My present writing enables me to record the lives of ten men who have left a noble mark on the national scene; yes, and the international scene too. Referring only to *men* (please excuse!), my choice in each case refers to those nurtured in the "little chapel" and freely deciding to go out "over the top" into turbulent situations, in faith, as a result of their beliefs. Compendiums of the good and brave and famous usually come from the pen of historians who have researched their subjects, I can only claim knowledge of my people "because I was there", at least in the formative years and by keeping up friendships with my heroes. Further. I know that in each case there was a *"higher presence"* with them and they went out "authorised" in a similar way to the experience of the explorer and missionary, David Livingstone, who, contemplating Christ's words recorded at the end of *Matthew's* gospel "I am with you always!", said: "it is the word of a perfect gentleman". Probably Frederick Mann's hymn verse denotes the attitude of the people of Banks Road Chapel:

> Things deemed impossible I dare,
>
> Thine the call and thine the care;
>
> Thy wisdom shall the way prepare,
>
> Thy will be done.

Six of my characters belonged to two families; each man differed in his channel of life as their personality was unique. However, their mutual blessings from stalwart parents undoubtedly contributed to their moral muscle.

The Rev. Dan Oakes, the Liverpool blacksmith became a christian martyr in Papua, New Guinea (1942).

CHAPTER I

William Daniel Oakes (1906 – 1942)

In his book, *One Hundred Years in the Islands,* NEVILLE THRELFALL refers to the work of Dan Oakes on four occasions and includes a photograph. The book is a history of the christianizing of the islands of New Guinea by the work of Methodists from Australia, and is a record produced for the Methodist/United Church in 1975 from the first missionary ventures in 1875.

Early missionaries suffered death at the hands of cannibals and in one of his letters to me of the 24th June 1935, Dan Oakes included a group photograph of about 30 of his students, indicating two of them whose grandfather; (using Dan's own words) "tortured and slew his enemies and ate their remains — who is actually known to have cut off the hand of a man and to have cooked and eaten it in front of the poor sufferer".

From the age of about 12 years Dan Oakes was my friend in Garston. A year older than me, he joined our Wesleyan Scout Troop in unusual circumstances. His family were Church of England and the boy, Willie, as his parents called him, was a chorister in the parish church. His home, 11 Stanley Street, was right by the Council School where we were both educated from the age of five to fourteen years. The Little Wesleyan chapel started a scout troop in June 1917, probably engendered by patriotism resulting from the Great War of 1914-18. After hostilities ceased we had a "peace treat' in the Council School for all the scholars and, gratefully, the teachers started an evening play-centre, as many parents and some teachers too, had lost their home influence with their lives. It seemed natural for the adjacent thriving Wesleyan scout troop (most of their boys were scholars), to be asked to form a branch of scouting in the play-centre. I was one of the small scouts who helped and Dan Oakes was one of the scholars who 'joined up'.

'Joined up' was an appropriate phrase for he entered into scouting so thoroughly that he became scoutmaster at the age of 19. But scouting was such an integrated part of youth work at the 'little chapel' that Dan Oakes soon became a Sunday School Teacher and prominant in all the good times enjoyed by teenagers. Leader of a teacher preparation class he also studied and became a Local Preacher of the Wesleyan Church, preaching in several churches of South Liverpool and urgently desiring to become a minister. But the educational merits of a council school product were not sufficient

The young Dan Oakes, wearing the original uniform of the 135th Liverpool Troop.

commendation for the Wesleyan ministry at the time, and the wage of an apprentice blacksmith insufficient to venture on theological studentship. But, in the providence of God, an Australian minister of the Methodist Church was combing British cities to secure candidates for the Australian ministry. Dan, along with another Liverpool candidate, was accepted and some twelve young men accompanied the Reverend D. C. HUGHES on a ship leaving Tilbury, London, on the 7th February 1928.

Naturally called 'The Twelve Apostles' by the crew, they had already started their training for the N.S.W. ministry. I accompanied Dan and Fred to Crewe on their London train, slighty sharing their trauma of parting, at Liverpool, with parents they would not see again. In Dan's case he faithfully wrote a daily record for years and sent it to his mother, as convenient. My weekly visit to his home kept me well posted with his experiences, in addition to the copious letters he sent me.

'Over the Top' was also his first experience on landing at Sydney for he was sent for twelve months as a missioner to BRAIDWOOD, a little outback town of 2,000 people, where he performed all the tasks of a minister over an area almost as large as an English county; naturally he started a scout troop — I have a snapshot of them.

Three years in a training college then followed, and, turned out as a probationer, he was allotted the Methodist circuit of MILTON, a seaboard area sixty miles long by twenty, and with nine churches he had to act as superintendent. As though that was not sufficient work and responsibility, after only twelve months he took on the challenge of becoming a missionary on the British islands of New Guinea.

This was 'Over the Top' again indeed; as a probationer he needed to serve three years before ordination and not to marry before then. However, the missionary need was so urgent that Dan was ordained as a Methodist minister on the 3rd March 1933, and he married MARION, the daughter of a Methodist minister, in the April. Forthwith they sailed for ULU Island in the Duke of York group, set between the main islands of New Britain and New Ireland. Let Dan himself tell us about ULU.

"Less than 60 years ago these islands had not been explored nor had any attempt been made at evangelization. The natives were all cannibals and, at the coming of the first missionary 58 years ago, lived in a state of complete savagery. Their dead buried inside houses and only barely beneath the surface; a man's death meant the strangulation of his wife, or wives. Every evil thing that we might conceive was the common rule among this people.

"This island of Ulu was uninhabited for it was the common feasting ground of all the people in other islands — the scene of all their cannibal orgies. Their common belief was that all the evil spirits resorted to Ulu and that there all who were evil must be executed. All their enemies were evil and were killed at Ulu and likewise those within the tribe who broke its laws were taken to Ulu to be slain. There is still present among these people the superstition that evil spirits lurk in Ulu. Whilst they will go to the Ulu Mission Hospital for aid in their time of sickness and also to the Mission schools for education, nothing can persuade them to make their permanent home on Ulu island. Even when it happens that one of them dies in the mission hospital, the relatives will always take the corpse to their own village for burial, for Ulu is the last place where they might desire to lie in death".

In my introduction I told of the cannibal grandfather of two of the youths in his schools. Dan had three schools on Ulu but there were others in his charge on the smaller islands. Readers of the book 'One Hundred Years in the Islands' have an early picture of tribal warfare and savagery. The schools which Dan Oakes continued to develop were indeed the antidote to the poison of tribal rivalry. Referring to the two grandsons, Dan wrote: "They have chosen to follow the *good* and they are the most outstanding of the younger teachers in that circuit". In addition to civilizing qualities and christian ethics, the scholars were taught agricultural skills, helping to maintain themselves by their own gardens and by the harvesting of coconuts, etc. Dan was responsible for the export of the products of 3,000 coconut palms. I quote the time-table of his central school at Ulu. "From 6.00 to 6.30 am physical jerks, lessons 6.30 to 8.00 am and 9.00 to 10.45; afternoons were usually spent in gardening, housebuilding, etc. On Wednesdays and Fridays the boys worked in the big gardens of the mission to aid mission expenses, and on other days in their own gardens growing produce for their own consumption. Games were not neglected and primitive cricket was a favourite".

Rainwater from the roofs of buildings had to be conserved in home-dug reservoirs, for the coral island had no natural water supply.

Dan's short apprenticeship as a blacksmith in a Garston factory and his practical scout training together with text books sufficed for him to tackle and supervise all kinds of jobs. But study remained his constant discipline and pleasure. Soon his success in Ulu island commended him for wider responsibilities and his next headquarters became PINIKIDU, across the BISMARK SEA and half-way up the 300 mile long island of New Ireland. From there his letters referred to his studies, translating into native tongues, and the 550 books of his personal library.

In a thirteen-page letter to me from Pinikidu he referred to his study in the thirty-year-old wooden house (with all dimensions) with a photograph of King George V on one wall accompanied by a picture presented to him on leaving his home church at Garston. It was of beautiful penmanship, a testimonial from all his Banks Road friends, inscribed by one of the friends in his group.

As from Ulu, he was continually sailing, using a whaler row boat and sometimes a Kelvin launch. Referring to one bad trip in his little cockleshell he said: "fortunately the rain was so heavy it helped to keep down the big waves" and on another occasion he was terrified in the dark and storm, having only his pocket compass for guidance. Again to quote him: "I think I could run a troop of sea scouts now!"

Besides being a sailor he was also a foot-slogger, usually alone. After one such sea journey he had to walk sixteen miles from the coast over a 3,000 foot range of hills to visit 14 of his villages. Once he covered 140 miles in twelve days.

I have not mentioned medical work. From Ulu Dan sent me a snapshot of himself operating on a patient upon an ordinary table, and Neville Threlfall's book says: "When the Rev. Dan Oakes began a seven-year ministry at Pinikidu in 1935, he and Mrs Oakes were able to develop an extensive medical work there".

Their first child, GEORGE, was born at Ulu in 1934 far from doctor or white associates; later PARKER was born in Australia. On their first furlough in N.S.W. in 1936, the couple had a very happy and useful six months after nearly four years on the mission field. Marion could stay at her parent's home in Sydney but Dan studied for two terms in Sydney University and did 'deputation' work which consisted of preaching and lecturing in suburban churches. Various gifts helped him greatly, for a lantern enabled him to project slides from his own photographs; a duplicator was to be useful, particularly for teacher training, and they also gave him a medical box for his patrol work.

Their second furlough, in November 1939, found Dan in much demand. The Australian Methodist Conference met in Sydney in February and he was the speaker to 2,000 people at the Conference 'Overseas Rally'. Six weeks of lecturing and preaching took him hundreds of miles and to twelve circuits.

When Oakes returned in 1936 from his first furlough Neville Threlfall reports that he asked the mission natives why they had not carried out, in his absence, his instructions concerning the gardens. They replied: "We didn't expect you back. Nobody has ever come back here before". But on his second return in 1940, the situation was vastly improved and Threlfall tells of visitors to New Ireland from Australia who were "delighted with the Church in the islands and with the signs of Christian joy, faith and friendship which they found in the people".

War Clouds

In a letter to me of the 8th July 1940 Dan, expressing anxiety about the war in Europe, continued: "All at home are constantly in our thoughts and prayers — especially in view of the grave danger to England now that France is in the hands of Germany". They little thought that Japan would attack Pearl Harbour and Singapore in December 1941; before the end of January both KAVIENG, chief town of Dan's New Ireland, and RABAUL of New England were in the hands of the Japanese hordes. Of course I received no letters and the last news came with the fleeing personnel and women. Marion and their two boys safely reached Sydney. The last news I had of Dan's whereabouts came from Marion, via his mother: "Dan, with a facial wound and refusing an escape boat, said he was going up-country to care for 'his boys'," but Marion had no firm news until Japan had lost the war.

Late in 1941 Dan Oakes had left Pinikidu for Kavieng in the north because they had no minister there; he also became the chaplain to the Australian forces there. Kavieng was the first to fall to the enemy who then took Rabaul, a town of New Britain, and the captives were taken there. On June 22nd over one thousand civilians, including ten Methodist missionaries (also Dan) were placed on a Japanese ship which, on the 1st July 1942, was sunk by a submarine, and all passengers lost their lives.

There was great mourning in Sydney when the grim fact became known after hostilities had ceased, and on Sunday, November 10th 1945, a service was held in the main Wesley Chapel to commemorate the ten martyrs who remained at their post of duty. At Dan's home church in Banks Road, Garston, Liverpool, a similar service, remembering Dan, was held on Sunday, October 18th 1945, in which I took part; the Rev. Harry Wakefield, himself a returned missionary from Africa, led the service.

Loss and Gain

Truly the annihilation of the entire white staff of the important mission field was a tragic loss and for Dan Oakes a terrible cost as a reward for his determined devotion. But even by human standards a careful reading of 'One Hundred Years in the Islands' would not leave the reader without hope or admiration. For methodists who could have read 'The Dossier' (N.S.W. Missionary Circular) for 15th November 1945, as it reported the Commemoration Service referred to, they would read a counterbalance to grief and loss. I quote a paragraph: "Before we entered the Chapel we knew that at least four widows had offered for service in New Guinea, and the four missionary nurses released from Japanese prison camps, emaciated in body and far spent but with souls unconquered, were eager for the front line again. The service proceeded, pitched to that high key of heroism".

The Anglican chaplain with the Rabaul garrison was refused his wish to travel on the ill-fated boat. He reported how the ten missionaries used to meet very early each Sunday to worship together before forced to their daily work, and that on the morning of their embarkation they read together the 107th Psalm. One of the widows, writing of that last morning, ended: "Henceforth let every Australian Methodist regard the 107th as the Psalm of the Methodist Missionary martyrs of 1942".

What of the indigenous christian islanders? In about 1936 I was teaching in Sunday School a class of 12 to 13-year-old English boys. I arranged for a couple of them to write to a couple of Dan's native boys at Pinikidu. Dan agreed and the letters were sent: TAMILU and EKONIA responded — I still have the letters and Dan's translations. Referring later to Tamilu (much older than my boys but, according to Dan 'of roughly similar standard'), he said Tamilu had progressed and is to be appointed as a tutor for our college. "Soon he will be nominated for the ministry, we hope".

Standing out specially in Threlfall's book, for me, is HOSEA LINGE "Oakes placed him at Pinikidu whilst he himself went to visit Kavieng Circuit". After the Japanese take-over there were several native teachers and ministers who braved all kinds of conditions, faithful to their Church and Christ. Linge carried on responsibilty for all the churches in a 'parish' of New Ireland, nearly 200 miles long including islands, and on foot. He is often referred to. How many of Dan Oakes' progeny were faithful and successful I do not know. The foreword of Threlfall's book is by BISHOP SAIMON GAIUS who was a scholar in the schools for which Dan was responsible. He was the first native candidate for the Methodist missions ministry who was sent to Australia, and was trained at Leigh College where a memorial plaque remembered an earlier student, Dan Oakes.

Growing up in Australia

Dan's eldest son, George, who has visited my home in Liverpool twice, became a native officer on the mainland of Papua New Guinea, and in a letter of 16.12.56 he told me a lot about his job. He had just completed a patrol of 65 days and he said: "The natives of this area have given up their head-hunting and cannabalistic desires". He visited 51 villages and took census of 10,000 natives. He was responsible for 40,000 in his area of 2,100 square miles. He had the powers of a magistrate and could gaol guilty people for up to six months. His snapshot of himself with five native men revealed him as the only one wearing any clothes. George and his partner worked closely with the christian missions for the health and wellbeing in the villages. In the course of time George took degrees in an Australian university which finally enabled him to be the accountant and trading officer of the district, until Papua New Guinea gained independence in 1974.

And so the 'loss' or 'gain' equation goes on. It is a truism the "the blood of the martyrs is the seed of the church". I would add that the church in Dan Oakes's case was the wide Church of Christ which knows no boundaries between the religious and the secular.

The young Dan Oakes I knew in Liverpool was ever a youth of quick and firm decision and with that quality of stickability which converts genius into success, he certainly deserves a prior place in accord with my book title "Over the Top". Not quite an extrovert, yet he was central in all our youth activities in the 'little chapel', a blend of serious purpose and smiling joy. I remember once, when he was very young and green in the pursuit which was to become his passion — overseas missions, he was verbally chastised by the leader of the Wesley Guild when Dan said to the meeting: "We should take the gospel to all the 'natives' and if necessary take our army to compel them to believe". The leader who 'put him right' was a lovely older gentleman, whom we all respected with the title of Pa Pearson. He had a flowing moustache and, strangely enough, he was the blacksmith to whom Dan was apprenticed at the local Bobbin Works.

Later, when Dan became acting scoutmaster (and I his assistant), he drove the boys on with such persistance that for several months we held the record in the Liverpool Southern Division for earning proficiency badges. When the call came to prepare for the Australian ministry he passed the scout leadership to me and studied more intensively. His father, being an ocean-going ship's engineer, was seldom at home. His mother, aunt, brother and sister did not want him to leave home and his mother tried to curtail his studies by turning the gaslight off at the meter. Dan persisted, using candle ends.

Dan's final service and sermon before embarking for Australia left a deep impression on the crowded congregation in the 'little chapel'. Many of Dan's workmates were there but when, in the past he hammered out hot metal in the works' smithy in Garston, he little knew of the refining fire which would become his lot. I guess that when he was welding tool heads on to shafts or handles, he was preparing for to join many souls to the Lord of his life which became his constant passion; and success, I think.

Chapter II

THE CONSTABLE/JONES FAMILY

Sydney John Constable (1900-1983)
Wilfred George Constable (1902-1976)

This local biography must include several members of one family who attended 'the little chapel under the bridge'. The early life of the family could more interestingly be read in the autobiography: 'Jack Jones, Union Man' (Collins, 1986). I must write from outside the family but from inside the friendship of its male members.

Jack Jones, known to me as Jim and christened Jim Larkin Jones, was step-brother to my great friend Sydney Constable, about whom I must write first. Jim's true older brother, Arthur, who went by the name of 'Biff' was my true contemporary by age, church membership and work, for we were both railway trainmen and also great friends of Dan Oakes, of the previous chapter.

Children are usually stirred by the sight of a uniformed man. At the age of 10 years I glowed when I repeatedly saw two men (teenagers really) in blue shorts, sailor hats and blue jerseys which boldly, in white, stated: SEA SCOUTS. They were home on leave from coastwatching duties. In the 1914/18 war, when manpower became very scarce, coastwatcher points reduced their trained staff and supplemented every man lost by two volunteer boy scouts. Sydney and Wilf Constable were the objects of my admiration. Syd, the elder, having a good friend Fred, combined with a church official Bill to start a church scout troop at the 'little chapel' in June 1917. Syd became Assistant Scoutmaster; the troop was entitled '135th Liverpool, Banks Road Wesleyan'. My two elder brothers joined and I tagged along even before I had attained the minimum age of 11. On the day before Armistice Day of November 11th, 1918, Syd Constable had his 18th birthday and H.M. King George V took him for two years to clear up the mess that the war had left. But before then Syd had taken me to camp and instructed me well in the rudiments of scouting. He was a very methodical and reliable young man. I was to learn his worth later.

On returning to Civil life Syd resumed his job with the London and North Western Railway at the steam shed of Speke Junction, near Garston, as an engine fireman. My father was a driver there and I joined them in 1923, the same year in which 'Biff' joined them. In course of time we were all riding on steam engines over the bridge that separated the 'under the bridge' community from the rest of Liverpool's suburb of Garston.

Fred, having completed his national service before Syd, now became scoutmaster and Bill, satisfied that the troop was well established, concentrated on church and choir, about which he was more knowledgable than scouting. With Syd's assistance the troop prospered and was a strong feature in church life; moreover we had some fine, happy times. Meanwhile Syd's brother, Wilf, junior by a couple of years, remained valuable to the troop until a strange happening.

Wilf Constable, wearing two medals for gallantry, being greeted by H.R.H. Prince of Wales (later King Edward VIII) in the presence of the Chief Scout, Robert Baden-Powell.

One day, boarding a ferry boat at Liverpool to cross the river, Wilf saw a man fall into the river, plunged in and saved him. For this he was awarded the Scout Bronze Cross for bravery, which we call 'the Scout V.C.', this led to interesting developments. (The Liverpool Shipwreck and Humane Society also awarded him their medal for gallantry).

Edward, Prince of Wales, after his 1914-19 war service, was very popular and took great interest in ordinary people. He had a particular interest in boy scouts and was a strong patron of the Movement. (I saw him in 1929 at the Arrowe Park, Birkenhead, International Scout Jamboree, when the Prince slept in a hike tent on the Hall front lawn and appeared with the Chief Scout, Baden-Powell). In the early years after the war, Edward embarked on some long visits to our countries of the 'Empire' and to America. In each case a scout 'guard of honour' saw him off and welcomed him back. These groups were usually 'King's Scouts' having earned the highest proficiency award. Wilf Constable not only qualified for this but also held the medal for heroism. On such an occasion at Portsmouth harbour, where the Prince embarked on H.M.S. Rodney, the heir shook hands with each of the youths, including Wilf.

On a very special welcoming occasion, many months later, the small welcoming group was enlarged and became a 'Posse of Welcome' (Baden-Powell arranged things like that). Again, Wilf was there and the Prince went straight to him, remembering his award, and the national newspapers made a front page photo of the event. Each time I visited the Jones/Constable home I saw the large photo

Sydney Constable, an early camping snapshot.

on the mantlepiece. I have another photograph of Wilf taken in Sydney harbour years later on his ship; Wilf Constable, in his engineer officer's uniform, posing on deck with my friend, Dan Oakes, the missionary: an interesting meeting on the other side of the world of friends from 'the little chapel under the bridge'. Yes, Wilf became a merchant seaman engineer officer and later a civil engineer in America, where he married and adopted American citizenship. My last information of him was in his post of Port Engineer-Surveyor, in New Orleans.

'Garston United!' Ship's Engineer Wilf Constable meeting the Rev. Dan Oakes (Chapter 1) on his ship in Sydney Harbour, Australia in 1930.

Returning to our chapel scout group, after this short memory of Wilf Constable, there came a time when we teenagers in the troop felt a little deprived because Syd and Fred had found the girls of their choice and vied, in good humoured argument, as to the respective merits of their sweethearts. Lacking the full time attention of our officers we underlings were probably thrown more on our own resources and sometimes we slacked off. It became worse when Sydney's position on the steam trains became more complex. He regretted absences but was always interested and helped with advice and encouragement: he continued to teach in the Sunday School. But worse was to follow, or was it *good?*

Syd's young lady was a member of the Parish Church, St. Michael's. Came the time when an enthusiastic curate, the Rev. Mulliner, wanting to start a troop at St. Michael's Church, needed the help of an expert: we *lent* him Sydney. Our troop was the 135th South Liverpool: Syd's became the 237th and started a forty-year success story for that group, for soon they had cubs, guides and brownies. We were happy for their success and it led to the time when Dan Oakes and I were taking responsibilities in the 135th. Sometimes competitors with the 237th, for sometimes Wesleyan boys joined them and sometimes C. of E. boys joined us (as indeed Dan Oakes had joined us six years earlier). Often we complemented each other, a few boys from either joining week-end or summer camp, according to the availability of 135th or 237th officers and camp grounds, for all the officers were industrial or office workers. Scouts often mixed at 'Association' training camps but the widest gesture of unity was when Dan and I, with Syd, arranged monthly church parades for all the Garston scout groups at each other's church venues. We had good relations with the 'Congoes' (Congregationalists) and one of our 135th patrol leaders, Fred Buckley, had started a troop at Bowden Road Presbyterian church, a mile beyond 'the bridge' boundary. This was happening at a time when 'Orange' and 'Green' communities and groups staged active religious opposition to each other, continually in our area, and Liverpool generally. The 135th always had a few Roman Catholic boys who joined with their school friends and this continued after a Catholic school and church were built 200 yards from our Wesleyan headquarters. (R.C. boys were never expected to attend our church parades). Looking back from the position in the present 1980's, when the Anglican Bishop of Liverpool, the Roman Catholic Archbishop, the Free Church Moderator and the Methodist Chairman are all in friendly co-operation, perhaps our youthful ventures in unity played a small part.

Continuing this vein of thought concerning Sydney Constable and myself, he gained great respect in St. Michael's church, attended their services with regularity, and encouraged all the 237th to faithfulness and bold belief. His uttered prayers were natural and occurred in every phase of scouting, at weekly parades, 'scouts owns' and camp fires, which usually closed with the hymn 'Glory to Thee my God this night', often sung as a 'round'. I think he blended the universality and fervour of the Wesleys' with the treasures and devotion of the Anglicans. However, during his leadership with the 237th (later re-numbered The 6th Allerton) two boys became C. of E. clergymen. But he remained a faithful Methodist up to the time of his death in

1985. As a matter of fact I delivered a Methodist 'class ticket' to him each year and in his later years continued to minister to him as his appointed 'class leader' and at the same time gained practical advice and encouragement from his down-to-earth beliefs.

About three or four times a year he attended our 'little chapel' service and often said he could not manage without the inward spur of 'coming home' which those visits gave him. One such visit was very poignant for he and Bella, his wife, were in deep trouble. Bella's sister was mortally ill, cancer I think. She had three infants and her husband was not reliable. Syd confided in me and, at the end of the evening service, he knelt at the communion rail in deep supplication; I knelt with him. His prayers were not answered in the way they desired, the mother died, but Syd and Bella took two of the little ones into their home and nurtured them for many years to adulthood, with great credit.

Syd had one son, Albert, and I remember Syd's broad, proud smile after returning from a private camping holiday; Bella and Syd on their tandem bike with the few-months-old Albert initiated into one of Syd's joys, camping. Albert became a worthy scout, 'Queen's Scout', and a good helper to his dad. Bella was quiet, demure, a firm christian and an excellent mother to Albert and her two motherless dependants. Sadly, she died about 8 years before Syd passed on at the age of 83.

As a railwayman, fireman and driver, Sydney Constable was exemplary; efficient, punctual and reliable. As a tradeunionist he was loyal, thoughtful and ever conscious of the problems of fellow-workers in the 24-hours-a-day responsibilities. He was not a trenchant reformer, like his brother, Jack Jones, for his speciality was scouting and youth training. My own voluntary T.U. activity at the depot could always depend on people like Syd to forward good schemes and advocate sound policies. Half-way through his driving career the bi-yearly medical test proved that his eyesight had fallen just below the accuracy required for main-line driving. To fail, I would have been most perturbed, but he took it philosophically and even put it to good effect in his increased availibity as a scoutmaster. He became a shed engineman and one on whom the foreman could rely to serve engines with all certainty and get them back into traffic 'on time'. He was able to take on wider scouting responsibilities for the local Association as his turns of railway duty became regular. The older branch of scouting. Rovers — aged 18 plus, required better organizing and Syd was made Assistant District Commissioner over that branch. During his long scouting career he earned the Medal of Merit *and bar* and the Chief Scout's special award of the Silver Acorn.

When Syd combined with the Rev. Mulliner to start the 237th, they rented a small field, adjacent to the Garston hospital and just beyond the railway bridge boundary. In the course of time Mr. Mulliner moved on to another parish and some anxiety began to develop lest the rented field, close to an expanding bus depot, might become lost as the scout headquarters. Unfortunately, Mr. Mulliner died in middle age, and his wife, who had kept in touch with Sydney (she had been the cubs' Akela), gave a gift of money so that the field could be purchased. Further money was raised and the field to this day is called 'The Mulliner Memorial Field', and it has been a boon to the Group, the Church, and the Allerton Scout Association (the modern name).

Such expanding responsibility and a new H.Q. building added to Syd's anxiety in later years, especially after retirement from the railway at the age of 65. Visiting him one day, he anxiously asked my advice on a problem; it was usually the other way about, me asking his advice. The vicar had urged him to become the church verger, to maintain, heat and be generally every-body-else, in the vast ancient church: should he, being a methodist, take on this official position? I urged him to do so, though the wage would be small. Thus started another phase of his life, serving with his usual thoroughness, until old age and failing eyesight caught up with him.

Scout Commemorative Seat to the memory of Sydney Constable. From left to right: The writer, Frank Mason; 3, Mabel Williams, Akela for 20 years, influencing characters in 'Over the Top'.

As age impaired his health, he went to live with his son and daughter-in-law, Albert and Mollie, at Widnes eight miles away. With a mutual friend, I sometimes visited him and was pleased to see him in such loving security. On the 18th October 1987 a fine seat was dedicated to his memory on the fringe of the ground and facing the headquarters where he spent almost a lifetime encouraging the youth of Garston — for he died in March 1983 aged 83. He spent his last few months in a pleasant nursing home, almost blind. I was able to spend some time with him. When his mind wandered a bit and broken sentences resulted, there was a typical earnestness to face a problem or achieve a result. Perhaps when I was with him, scouting times came to the fore: "We will have to get a bit of something good for their dinner, they need it, you know, Frank"! Yes, Syd was always wanting to give Garston youth what they needed!

Jack Jones: slum child who became the famous leader of the Transport and General Workers Union.

Chapter III

THE CONSTABLE/JONES FAMILY
(Continued)

Arthur Constable Jones (1907-1987)
James (Jack) Larkin Jones (1913-   )

In later life I had less to do with the Jones' side of the family than with my friend, Sydney Constable. Syd and Wilf, with their elder sister, had been born in a fine house at Mostyn, North Wales, overlooking the estuary of the River Dee. Their sea-faring father had risen to be a customs officer at the time of his death. The fortunes of their widowed mother therefore had declined and she gravitated to the four-roomed house in Garston where I knew them. There she maintained a poor living by keeping lodgers, mostly dockers, who in those days lived themselves on the poverty line. In the course of time she married one of her lodgers, Mr. Jones. Church and scoutwise I grew up with Arthur Jones, Jack's elder brother, called 'Biff', even by his mother. Another great friend of mine was named Walter and he, too, had a family nickname, 'Squib'. Biff and Squib were particular friends and a couple of clowns together, but staunch christians and good scouts, as teenagers.

Biff somewhat disappeared from the scene at the age of about eighteen for, made redundant at the engine shed, he was transferred to Widnes and there he married; they linked up with the Salvation Army. Their first child, David, was a mongol and continued totally dependent: a handicap indeed for his parents as well as David. As William, their second child grew, his ambition was to aid, perhaps to heal his brother. He trained as a doctor with great credit to his humble and disadvantaged parents, and became a clever cancer specialist. Dr. William Jones is at present the cancer specialist at the teaching hospital at Leeds and connected with Leeds University.

Father Arthur (Biff) may not graduate to my list of remarkable and famous men by virtue of his son William's prominence, any more than his mother, who gave birth to and nurtured Syd and Wilf and Jack. But 'Biff' and his mother were typical of the strong stock grounded firmly in 'little chapels' and small communities. From their strong beliefs and faithful love are born the strong oaks and fragrant roses that delight our imagination and strengthen us all.

At Christmas 1987 I had occasion to send a Christmas card to Jack Jones. he had taken the trouble, in his busy life, to call at my home a month earlier and during some friendly banter I had referred to one of our Lord's commands. Jack, smiling, had said: "Yes! Jesus is *reputed* to have said that" and I made a suitable reposte. So with my Christmas card I included a short note, writing: "I faintly remember, Jim (his correct name), sitting by you on a Sunday School form, telling you about Grenfell of Labrador and Livingstone in Africa as, in danger, he recollected that Jesus had said:"I will be with you always"! and concluded: "it is the word of a gentleman". Jim's card, in reply, was an imposing House of Commons picture with his written pleasure at our meeting and he remembered Livingstone and Grenfell; also that he ranked his brother, Syd, as an example of the best christian people and (generously) ranked me with Syd. A compliment indeed!

Jack Jones had squeezed his visit to my home in between public engagements in Liverpool and a visit to the 6th Allerton scout headquarters to see, and meditate, on the commemoration seat bearing his brother's name, to which I referred earlier.

On his visit we were delighted to speak of characters reared at the "little chapel'. I value very much his book, published in 1986, about his extra-ordinary life, and his kind written appreciation on the front page. With his permission I can recall some of the landmarks in his life, embracing them in his family in the context of our 'little chapel' and his birthplace 'under-the-bridge'.

I can verify the early pages of his autobiography, the family home in York Street, poor and cramped, in a long terraced row. Was York the name of a cathedral or of a cathedral city? There was Durham, Canterbury and Lincoln Streets to keep it company and in declining prosperity of inhabitants. Durham Street faced a little park and seldom saw barefooted children, but Jack shared domicile in York Street with rats, mice, cockroaches and bugs in common with the factories adjoining. Each street of more than a hundred houses crouching together, met the main artery shopping street, Window Lane, and with similar streets flanking the other side. Cathedral or city? Saints and sinners, the 'little chapel' ministered to all and sundry.

My two brothers worked in the factories and the 'bobbin works' was the largest in Britain, supplying textile mills all over the world. Banks Road 'Wessies' had more than their foot-in-the-door, for several of the bobbin works' foremen and managers held office in our church and most of our congregation were as closely connected as miners are in a mining village.

I reminded Jack, on the occasion of his visit, that the last time I had seen him, before he became a permanent trade union offical, was from my shunting engine on the dockside as he was checking the loading of bananas from ship into vans with destination for the north, south, east and west of Britain.

In early Sunday School and scout days, I had remembered Jack (Jim) as a pale, slim, thirteen-year-old recovering from a bout of rheumatic fever. the next time I actually met him was when, as a young city councillor, he was tall and huskey, broad and genial. I will not try further to recall in detail his progress to that point: read the book, it is very like the man!

In general I would say that Jack's main attribute was that he was constantly dealing with individual workmen on a *personal level.* He knew their thinking, qualities, faults and weaknesses, and dealt with them on that basis. Often, in his book, he refers to leaders, politicians and statesmen of all parties as not actually *knowing* the people with whom they were dealing.

He remembered, more personally than I remembered, the degradation of the docker (he and his father were dockers) who had to stand in a pen at the dock gates beseeching a foreman to take him on for a day's work. Perhaps he had not worked last week, perhaps he looked too frail for the heavy loading in ships holds, perhaps he had not bought a pint for the foreman last evening. Jack was human, a negotiator and a realist, who knew that not all his opponents were on the management side of problems.

Jack had missed the benefit of a few teenage years in the company of his fellows in scouts, Sunday school and church life. He did come to scouts and even had a try at Sunday school teaching but, when quite a juvenile, he took office in his tradeunion branch. The accounts in his book of early childhood make moving reading. The continual poverty and the hard work of his mother to provide, with father unemployed. The general sickness of children and the deaths resulting. The desparation and drinking of adults and his mother's part in settling quarrels; all burned into his consciousness and, no doubt, as freedom literature came into his hands, he became a much more serious boy than we, who enjoyed the privileges of more secure lives. For years he could not get established in a secure job as he studied at night-school and tried not to become just a casual worker on the docks; but that became his fate as unemployment was rife. It involved him in strong tradeunion activity and, at the time of the national scandal of the 'means test' he led a march of 2,000 Liverpool unemployed to the Houses of Parliament in 1934: he was only about 20 years of age.

Jack was elected as a Liverpool city councillor, expanded his tradeunion activity, met Ernie Bevin and many leading politicians, and became a member of the International Brigade, opposing the excesses of General Franco in Spain. He had a semi-official role in Spain but fought in one of the great battles and was wounded. Back in Liverpool, convalescing, he worked hard with relief schemes for his Spanish comrades and impoverished families, being helped by several business leaders in Liverpool who feared the growing Nazi menace. At this time he married Evelyn whose husband had been killed in Spain. Jack tells how, in due course, he was speaking at a meeting where Ernie Bevin was the principal attraction. Bevin was concerned when 'young Jones' received a message, evidently distracting him from the business of the meeting. Discovering the contents of the message Bevin said: "You'd better be getting along!" for Evelyn had given birth to their first child, Jack, in Mill Road hospital.

Closely following this happy event, came news that Jack had won the appointment to become the T.G.W.U. district organizer in Coventry for the Midlands. I remember his brother Syd telling me this with much enthusiasm. In the Midlands the motor car construction industry was growing and Jack was very successful in negotiation and in attracting thousands of new members to the Transport and General Workers Union. Merseysiders were reluctant to lose him but they kept in touch with him and sometimes T.U. friends stayed in their modest home. Commenting on the promotion, Jack, in his book, said that the wage was less than he earned on the dockside and to leave their two-roomed flat, with baby and meagre funds, did not at first please Evelyn. existing in lodgings for a time in Coventry, Evelyn herself found a roomy flat for 21 shillings weekly. Jack's thoroughness in Coventry seemed to lay the foundation for his eventually becoming the national assistant and the general secretary of the largest tradeunion in Britain. he hurried around his large Midlands area and, in some of the new small industrial firms, he virtually acted as the branch shop steward. I looked carefully in Jack Jones' autobiography for any communistic leanings or complicity, for their paths often crossed during negotiations. I wish I could say that Christ was his complete example and the Holy Spirit his driving power. He makes no such claims but his human compassion, still evidenced long after his retirement, in his voluntary work for the unemployed and pensioners, along with his life-long care for the underdog, satifies me as to where his heart has always been.

A great friend of mine in the 'little chapel', a sober but keen evangelist, who brought up a large family in the next street to where

Jack lived under similar conditions, wrote to him at about the time of his retirement at 65. My pal, Alf, showed me the reply to his own expressions of faith in Christ. Jack, thanking him and recognising his sincere beliefs, said (in effect): "those qualities you commend in christianity are the qualities I practise and admire in socialism". I truly believe Jack and regret the ease with which people of lesser stature can dismiss his motives to the communist level. But, as I commend him as a product of the 'little chapel', I have in my mind his mother and older brothers and that 'God moves in mysterious ways, His wonders to perform".

In November 1940 Jack's new home town was *'conventrated'* by German bombers, adding a new horrific word to our dictionaries. Germany had concentrated all their bomber strength to wipe out Coventry, which was central to Britain's production of war weapons, and the incendiary bombs which set the whole city ablaze were made for Germany in Coventry before the war started. Jack's flat was a casualty and his story relates their dangerous, frantic actions during the blitz. The wartime greatly affected workers' conditions and many firms had licence to dismiss staff without any negotiation, notice or recompense. Comparatively few were tradeunionists. Jack has many stories to relate. His strong points were for consultation and negotiation.

As the years went by his successes were rewarded by the T.G.W.U. who appointed him as district secretary at the age of 43, with close association with the general secretary in London. When Frank Cousins was the general secretary, he found in Jack an active partner and, having an assistant secretary in Harry Nicholas, promoted Jack also to that level in London's Transport House. During Cousins's appointment to the Government Cabinet in 1965, Jack virtually acted as the T.G.W.U. chief. I have said 'read the book' if you wish to wonder at the intensity and breadth of Jack Jones's activities in the higher responsibilities of tradeunion leadership. His influence over national labour policies earned for him, in a BBC gallop poll, the title of the 'most powerful man in Britain'. Probably the most lasting of his efforts on behalf of British trade unions was the establishment of A.C.A.S. (Advisory, Conciliation and Arbitration Service) in 1974, which to this day remains the means to bring Management and Unions together beyond the point of stalemate. Proposing the scheme in the New Statesman newspaper, he pressed government ministers and the T.U.C. until the scheme was set up. Invited to be its first chairman, he elected rather to continue in the service of his T.G.W. union. A book could be written also of his wide interest in international affairs and his useful visits to so many countries.

Protesting with pensioners, 1985.

Signing Standard Motors' wages agreement, November 1948.

Though he claimed no church membership nor denomination, he often worked closely with church leaders in this and other countries, occasionally speaking from their pulpits.

Many awards crowded on him, particularly in the latter years of his tradeunion general secretaryship. He said that he valued none more than the gold medal of the T.G.W.U., his own union. Prime ministers, Wilson and Callaghan, offered him knighthoods in vain. Told that he should accept some recognition from the nation and that a 'Companion of Honour' decoration would confer no title and no privileges he yielded to the pressure. On several occasions he had audience with the Queen, which he much appreciated, even accepting a verbal 'smack on the wrist' from her when she told of a cold period in the palace when a heating oil supply lorry refused to cross *his* T.G.W.U. picket line.

I wrote congratulations from the 'little chapel' concerning the Companion of Honour award, to which I shall refer when we consider another notable product of early years, but on that occasion Jack sent me, with his thanks, a copy of his 'Dimbleby Lecture' of December 1977, entitled: *The Human Face of Labour.*

Jack was often the butt of the national daily papers: I like to smile at the six-verse parody aimed at him by R. Woddis of the New Statesman. I give the first and last verses:

Speak gently to your kind boss,
Avoiding sudden rages;
It doesn't help to make him cross,
When seeking higher wages.

Show him how well you understand,
Regard him as your neighbour;
And shake him warmly by the hand,
When you withdraw your labour.

Now retired for about ten years, Jack Jones is still a busy man. When he called at my home recently, with his elder brother Syd's son and his wife, with whom he was temporarily staying, the two middle-aged good folk were content to sit during the precious half-hour that Jack was sparing me. But the substantial feet of Jack were firmly on my carpet and he talked with all the personality of his presence. I have said that, as a young teenager, he was quite puny and the slum residence of his home quite unlikely to provide a balanced diet with adequate vitamins, yet the family produced dynamic characters. I have said that the eldest, my friend Syd, was my fellow workman on steam engines. If you were in camp with him he had you out of the tent and running round the field, sloppy with heavy dew, each morning. He was a total abstainer of alcohol from choice and by example. He showed his physical endurance in the last ten years (up to 65) of his railway life for, whilst steam drivers had left behind the heavy firing duties that had taxed them severely, Sydney, because of his eyesight failure, remained a shed engineman which was very hard indeed, physically: endlessly climbing up steep footplate steps and struggled with handbrakes and stiff controls.

Wilf Constable had shown his swimming prowess by saving the man in the river but he was also a good footballer and had trials with the first division team, Everton.

Perhaps it would be right to conclude that right vitamins and even inherited physique were not the only factors in the family's drive and pre-eminence. Undoubtedly, the 'little chapel' had something to do with it.

Footnote: Since writing I was privileged to talk to an old lady, born and bred in Stanley Street. Living at number 15 she verified that Dan Oakes (chapter one) lived at number 11 and Fred Green (chapter nine) at No. 7 and that she often witnessed Mrs Constable/Jones passing her house to attend the Wesleyan church. The mother from York Street could take a direct route from home via narrow side-passsages across four streets of house of ascending prosperity. Stanley Street then became her direct route from *slum* to the ecstasy of methodist worship and friendliness.

The Rev. W. G. E. Treggenna-Piggott, O.B.E., RN.
Auxiliary Chaplain, Deputy Mayor of Plymouth.

Chapter IV

Bill Piggott (1904 – 1979)

The Wesleyan Circuit of chapels in South Liverpool could not provide a minister for the 'little chapel under-the-bridge', but varying supervision was afforded; most of the services were led by local preachers (laymen and women). Some shopkeepers and local tradesmen, hardly more prosperous than the dock and factory workers, served the chapel very faithfully and one such shopkeeper, a local preacher, had a son, WILLIAM PIGGOTT.

Billy Piggott came through the Sunday School and, aged about 13, joined the scout troop. Such boys could afford the simple uniform of a khaki jersey and blue shorts earlier than the average, whose sixpence-per-week delayed their much desired finery. Billy, therefore, was doubly welcome to enhance the lure of parade night. I think he was about 17 when he moved south with his parents, but Bill kept in touch with his special friends.

Their new home in a village near Bedford also provided a continuing place in the family of the Wesleyan Church, and in 1925 the Amptill circuit accepted the young man as a potential Wesleyan minister. His training at the Handsworth theological college, Birmingham, quickly revealed a bent he had shown earlier among the teenagers at 'Banks Road' and his first appointment after training took him among naval cadets and young people.

At the navy establishment, H.M.S. Ganges at Harwich, his future life with seafarers was determined. Moving further south to Chatham Garrison he became a naval chaplain and his first sea-going post was on H.M.S. Sheffield at a time when the 1939 war was looming. I have little record of his varied experiences on H.M. ships during the war until the end of Japanese hostilities when his ship sailed into Tokio harbour with the victorious American navy. Next they relieved Nagasaki, the site of the exploding of the second atomic bomb in August 1945. The complete devastation caused by the first bomb at Hiroshima was not fully duplicated at Nagasaki because of the contour of the ground. On one side the railway station remained intact and as the trains brought in the released British prisoners Bill Piggott was the first Britisher to receive them. The ghastly sight of annihilation of a city, witnessed by Bill, was hardly more than the tragic condition of most of the released men. Taking them home was a daily continuation of the horror and funerals at sea, a tragic reminder to the chaplain as he conducted the services.

Before Japan entered the war, Piggott's ship called at New Zealand. In our little Liverpool chapel the name of New Zealand had a romantic ring in my limited experience as a young scholar; also for young Billy Piggott. Each year, at the Sunday School anniversary, the secretary speaking from the front, would produce from his pocket an envelope announcing: 'I have something from New Zealand! there is a letter, I wonder who it is from?' the scholars knew; it was an annual appearance. Next, as he unfolded the letter: 'Here is something else, what can it be?' We all knew it was a one-pound note and that it was from the AKED family. half the family were still faithful workers here but equally faithful were the emigrants who remembered their own upbringing on this special Sunday School occasion (incidentally, one pound was half the weekly wage of a labourer in that earlier part of the 20th century). The reader will appreciate the happy reception given to Bill by those Aked folk so many years later in their New Zealand homes, a recollection also of many spreading influences of the 'little chapel' that cannot be recorded.

Most of the Rev. Bill Piggott's home leave occurred at Plymouth, causing increasing friendships and becoming a popular preacher in Methodist churches. There, also, he married Nancy Summerton in 1934. Doubtless his busy life and popularity in Plymouth prevented visits to Garston until, in wartime, the important port of Liverpool must have been visited by his ship and he was able to preach at his native 'little chapel' on the occasion of the chapel anniversary in March 1943. What a fabulous occasion it was! All seating and standing room occupied by the British Legion branch, naval cadets, scouts and guides, in addition to the 'regulars' and sundry Garston friends. only then did we appreciate his magnetism and fervency; a powerful voice and happy appeal. I am sure it was a special thrill for him, also.

Thirty-five years later, in a letter to me of October 1978, occurred the following sentence: "I am now celebrating 50 years in the Ministry and as a token of my gratitude for a wonderful experience, and in thanksgiving for the true foundation I received at 'Banks Road' I would like to give the Church a pound for every year of my Ministry".

As far as I know he only maintained regular correspondence with one Garston person, that was a teenage friend of his Banks Road days; it continued up to the time of Billy's death. I am obliged to that friend for a little of the information of the middle years. The Piggott family acquired, at some time, the additional surname

TREGGENNA and in the Navy he was known as Rev. W. G. E. Treggenna-Piggott.

Returning to his early naval times, Bill became noted as the founder and editor of the *Naval Magazine* (the official Naval newspaper), and as his career matured onward toward retirement he became *Port Chaplain for the British Sailors' Society;* he founded the *Fishermans' Protection Society,* was Chairman of the *League of Friends of the Plymouth Hospital* in addition to answering 'special calls on account of his popularity as a preacher and the inspirer of youth.

On retirement from the navy Bill Piggott became, in 1957, the minister of a Plymouth church, remaining there for eleven years in spite of the usual Methodist method of moving on their clergy each three years; additionally, he became the Superintendent of Plymouth's group of Methodist churches. On official retirement as a minister he remained in the same circuit of churches for a further four years as a supernumary and aid to the remaining ministerial staff.

Not content with christian work within the churches and his several remaining naval attachments, he stood for election to the City Council and served for nine years as a councillor. On one occasion when Queen Elizabeth made a state visit to Plymouth Bill was elected Deputy Mayor. But he held down, also, the national office of *Chairman of the National Joint Council for Civic Manual Workers,* having responsibility to negotiate wages and conditions for more than a million workers in our towns and cities. He made this fact an interesting factor of diversion from another national officer of Banks Road vintage, as I must explain.

In the year 1978 our *Banks Road Church Council* considered the distinction afforded to ex-members of our 'little chapel' in the award by the Queen of the *Order of the British Empire* to Bill Piggott and the *Companion of Honour* to Jack Jones, and I was commissioned to send our congratulations. Jack Jones expressed his appreciation of my message and sent to me a copy of the Dimbleby Lecture that he had delivered to the nation in the previous December. His letter had an Isle of Man postmark, where he was attending a conference, and also enclosed was a set of I.O.M. stamps, a special issue to commemorate John and Charles Wesley.

Equally, Billy was pleased and in his letter of 25th March 1978 he said: 'It is strange that Jack Jones and I are remembered (by Banks Road) because we have both pursued our careers in labour relations, he on the Trade Union side and I on the Employers. For apart from me being responsible for every employee of the Plymouth

Corporation of several thousands, I am now the *Chairman of the National Joint Council for Manual Workers,* of whom there are $1^1/_2$ million, and chief negotiator for their pay and conditions of service. This takes me to London, weekly — however it is good to have good health and plenty to do'. The letterheading of his notepaper bore the imposing British Sailors' Society emblem and the names of prominent patrons, headed by the Queen and Queen Mother, whilst below a name that the 'little chapel' could be proud of:

COUNCILLOR THE
REVD. W. G. E. TREGGENNA-PIGGOTT, O.B.E., R.N.
AUXILIARY CHAPLAIN

Sadly, my next letter to Plymouth was one of condolence and sympathy to his widow for, in the August of the next year, 1979, he died — laid low since preaching at Easter by a terminal illness. Nancy's reply witnessed to his courage and faith, uncomplaining.

Bill's wartime experiences on several ships would have made interesting reading had the details been available to me, but his widow has now forwarded me with one lovely story of continuing interest.

In the year 1940 Bill served on the River Clyde in Scotland with *armed* Merchant Cruisers; merchant ships commissioned and sent to patrol the North Sea. A former Canadian Pacific Line boat became the HMS Forfar and the good burghers of the Scottish town of FORFAR adopted the ship and commissioned a ship's ensign to be made of silk, which was presented to the ship's company.

Bill attended the service and ceremony in the town's parish church but, as occurred too often, the good FORFAR was sunk. Then followed a memorial service for the ship's company and later the bereft ENSIGN was entrusted to the care of Bill himself. Throughout his future ministry Bill used the White Ensign as a cloth for the Communion Table.

Years after Bill's death, Nancy approached the Admiralty and then the people of Forfar and an arrangement was made. Accompanied by their grandson, Nancy attended a simple ceremony and gave back into the keeping of the town the treasured White Ensign. Subsequently the honoured couple attended in the same parish church as guests at the service where the plaque in memory of the ship was shown. The flag is now treasured in the local museum and, Nancy said: "I was presented with a lovely book of remembrance".

Sometimes in our churches and private contemplation, we look back at Gospel-time miracles and wish that Jesus was walking our streets today. Yet we are surrounded by a 'crowd of witnesses', proving that the meek *do* inherit the earth and the pure in heart *do* see God; even members of little chapels.

Chapter V

THE GOODALL FAMILY

Doctor David Goodall (1940 –)
M.R.C.S., L.R.C.P., M.R.C.O.G.

The 'little chapel' was often the haven for *large* families of children, particularly in the first half of this present century. Remembering that families of three girls and three boys were not uncommon, my particular memory was of several *boys* of some families, particularly when the eldest boy proved to be 'a little imp'. As a leader or teacher became aware that the younger brother of their particular 'imp' was now in the lower Sunday school department, threatening to come up next year, and that very likely a tiny toddler was already contemplating the opportunity of maintaining family traditions, the said teacher either bridled with future fear or thrilled at the challenge.

Our voluntary staff, bone and marrow of the community of the large families, did not entirely relish the logic of parents of the large families who thankfully waved goodbye to their errant offsprings, Sunday-school-wards, so they could enjoy a Sunday afternoon snooze. In this regard the school was a social blessing even though the christian virtues only partially affected the children. Some of them, indeed, became a credit to their family and school but the best qualities resulted where the parents were also in the *team* of the 'little chapel', as with high ideals and caring efforts they saw through to success both the little imps and the little angels.

The Goodall Family were of this noble breed. The principle son I want to write about would even now not totally disregard the title of 'little imp' during the decade of the 1940's. For a local monthly news journal I wrote recently: "In the summer of 1949 a small wolf-cub of the 20th Allerton (Banks Road Methodist Group) was travelling to his first camp. The after-war years were frugal and the little home-made trek-cart proved to be both a blessing and a near tragedy. As our party neared the camp site, near Hatchmere, David Goodall's little legs gave out and we perched him precariously on top of the overloaded vehicle. To negotiate a steep hill we raised a fierce gallop, shouting boastfully but, at maximum speed, the wheels jammed, the cart stopped, and David (in what became a lifelong trait) kept on.

"He alighted less gracefully than an Olympic long-jumper, and, as he dabbed a bloody knee with his hanky, stifling ready tears, he actually predicted his future life of binding up wounds to save life.

"Doctor David Goodall became a missionary doctor in India for thirteen years and, returning in 1980 he resumed in Liverpool as a distinguished gynaecologist. Last month (1986) he moved house to Blackburn for the hospital desired his special skills and knowledge of Asian languages and people".

I remember him, as an older cub, stealing the show at our annual concert when his 'cub six' mimed 'Lord Ullin's Daughter', a Scottish poem and tragedy which ended with bride and bridegroom (David) perishing in the stormy waves; their boat an upturned school form. He became a capable scout, an asset at 'camp fires' and his enthusiasm and leadership capabilities were well used up to the point of him becoming assistant scoutmaster. He had the additional advantage, or misfortune, to have as his scoutmaster his own father. (Temporary misfortune akin to others whose parents certainly did not discriminate in their favour).

The Goodall parents were devoted chapel people and youth workers, as their parents and grandparents before them; on marriage they emigrated a mile away from under-the-bridge but remained faithful to the 'little chapel'. David was born whilst his father was abroad in the army fighting the 1939/45 war. Arthur and Elsie also took upon themselves a family responsibility when newly married, for Elsie's mother had died and schoolgirl sister Joan became as their daughter. Breaking my rule in these stories of young *men,* it is with pleasure I report Joan's useful life as she became a young woman. A valuable youth leader and teacher in the chapel, she attained the office of *National President of the Methodist Association of Youth Clubs* for the year 1963, among other attainments.

Meanwhile as David matured he became teacher and later leader of the senior department of the Sunday school. This led in turn to local preaching around the eight Methodist churches of South Liverpool. Similar to his 'auntie Joan' he rose to national regard and became the *Liverpool Youth Delegate to the Conference of the World Council of Methodist Churches* in Oslo, Norway, in 1961. Educated at the Holt Grammar school, he prepared to enter the medical profession at Liverpool University, for at an early age he had decided to become a medical missionary.

David was popular with many people and whilst he was at University they became anxious (not least of course his parents) when medical studies seemed to be secondary in the young man's priorities. He so loved scouting and sport, and was particularly friendly with Jackie Jackson of the Sunday school and church. Whilst still at the Holt school he excelled in athletics and at the local Scout Association's Annual Sports Day he was awarded the *Victor Ludorum* trophy as being superior to about 200 entrants in running and jumping. He was a natural leader among fellow scouts and a great camper. An interesting amateur film was made of his expedition to the Isle of Skye leading about ten senior scouts.

The annual *Scout Gang Show at London's Olympia* was a popular rage at the time and David Goodall had to emulate them by a Gang Show annually for our scout group in the church hall. Remembering his mimicry prowess as a young wolf-cub he successfully contributed each year and I remember remarking, during his medical student days, that his singing with a fellow scout, of 'The Bold Gendarmes' was as good as I had ever heard on the concert stage.

Of course he passed his medical finals and his adventurous wings were severely trimmed as his hospital training in various Liverpool hospitals progressed. Extremely long hours of duty and responsibility were almost diabolical training for what was to be his lot for many years in still harder conditions. At last he was accepted by the Methodist Missionary Society for service overseas as a medical missionary. To his delight it became clear that he would have to serve in Kenya, Africa, and his eyes lit up with joy as he contemplated climbing the magnificent Kenya mountain. But it was not to be.

Meanwhile his experiences in Liverpool hospitals matured, his speciality being gynaecology. But his interest in the 'little chapel' remained paramount (sometimes he preached) and Jackie's frequent presence and friendship in the church tied evermore firmly their allegience to the foundation for their further adventures.

Personally, I treasure a memory of this time for I was able to spend several days at the annual scout troop camp at Bala, North Wales, in the summer of 1966. David's father organized and led the camp. Both David and I had complexities of employment which prevented us being present at the camp from the first. Fortunately, our importunity coincided with the desire of our Akela to visit the camp where most of the grown scouts, including David, had been her charges from wolf-cub days. Mabel Williams therefore drove us to Bala and both the company and the topics of conversation on the way were really memorable.

Also abiding in my memory of the camp were the camp-fire occasions as the fire, from our elevated site above the lake, extended its glow from the twenty-plus happy faces down to the town lights glowing below on the darkening scene. David was an expert in camp-fire techniques and popularity, and we had a traditon of calls and cries, plus the favourite choruses; also, the sincere words spoken were worthy of the vast vault of our evening mountain cathedral.

David's schoolgirl sweetheart had become his wife and had borne him a son. Now Jackie was fully involved with all his activities and when the news came that they must go to Bengal in India, instead of Kenya, she had to prepare as intensively as David. March 1967 came and David, now 27 years of age, was a competent doctor of several Merseyside hospitals' experience. On the 19th they were to leave Liverpool for India. The 19th was a Sunday and half the congregation of the 'little chapel' were at Liverpool Lime Street station to see Jackie and David off by the 2.00 pm train to London. At London they were met by a 'Banks Road' friend of their early days at the 'little chapel', Fred Green, who you may remember started the scout troop in far off 1917. I treasure the consciousness that now, 50 years on, Fred was harvesting the fruit lightheartedly sown many years before this fine couple were born. Good fortune also that they were entertained in London by a Methodist doctor and his wife who had served in the hospital at *Sarenga,* David's destination.

A Re-dedication Ceremony on the completion of hospital extensions as Doctor David Goodall, superintendent of the Sarenga Mission Hospital, North India, stands behind the Bishop of Calcutta. The third figure is the building foreman responsible for the substantial extensions; he had previously been a leprosy in-patient.

Travel to India, starting the next morning, was via Paris, and by train to Trieste, then by boat to Bombay with calls at Venice, Brindisi, Port Said, Djibouti and Karachi, with many opportunities for sight-seeing. At Bombay the crunch came, with its humid heat, dust and dirt, and a first crushing appreciation of the extremes of wealth and poverty which they were to witness everywhere. Next, for a day-and-a-half, the train took them to Karagbur, 60 miles from the Methodist hospital at Sarenga. At the linehead they were welcomed by fellow-missionaries who loaded them into a landrover. There were two doctors, the present and past superintendents of the hospital, two ministers experienced at Sarenga, and a senior nursing sister of the hospital who they had met in England twelve months earlier; an excellent welcome!

David and Jackie were not to remain at Sarenga during the intense heat, for arrangements had been made for them to go to Darjeeling, far to the north of Calcutta, for language and other training in cooler circumstances. Before that additional journey, they stayed for a week at the hospital in the care of the Rev. David Hindle, and little Paul Goodall, now a very active four-year-old, enjoyed the company of their host's baby daughter. Throughout the long journey from England, Paul had been a great attraction to many as evidenced in David's interesting letters back to his church friends. At Sarenga he was particularly noticeable for his light blond hair and his aptitude to play vigorously with the roughest brown youngsters.

Their journey to the cooler north, welcomes and interests must be passed over to enable the hospital and work at Sarenga to be portrayed. On their initial arrival the hospital staff had garlanded Jackie and David with flowers and later they were similarly welcomed at the Methodist church and presented with a Bengali New Testament. Well situated, the hospital buildings were in good condition and adequate but much overcrowded with patients. On David's first day that he helped with the out-patients he needed Iris, the nursing superintendent, to translate from Bengali for the 150 needing daily attention, and found that of nearly 100 in-patients many had no bed but the floor.

There was no running water or electric current, save for the X-ray's tiny generator. David's letters tell of the delivery of babies by the light of paraffin storm lanterns and operations by the light of a pocket torch. Came the time when Jackie had her second child, Mark, in February 1968 and David's letter continued: "By the great deliverer!" a hark back to Liverpool times when grateful new 'mums' often praised his qualities by notices in the city newspapers and sometimes called down the blessings of named saints upon his curly head.

I (the writer) was pleased to hear a tribute to David over the local Merseyside radio, twenty years after his early days in Liverpool's Broadgreen Hospital. The radio 'ring-in' programme was considering the national subject of shortage of cash and staff in Britain's hospitals and a local statement of the *carelessness* of doctors. A local caller rebutted that slur for she, and her husband, had benefitted from the devotion of doctors in Broadgreen hospital. Speaking on Monday, 6th March 1988, she added: "Twenty years ago I was in Broadgreen hospital and a young doctor was most caring for an old lady who was very ill. Throughout the nights he visited her continually and as he was notable in serving the wards throughout each day I wondered if he ever got any rest. I believe he became a missionary and went off to India, or somewhere!" The last sentence rivetted my casual attention; no names were known, or mentioned.

Continuing the Indian part of the story:

An Indian doctor maintained the hospital until David and Jackie returned from their visit to Darjeeling, but had to leave before David (languageless) could become established. It was arranged for an old Indian medico to come in because he had previously served at Sarenga, but he died within a few months at the hospital which he had faithfully served in the past, leaving David as the only doctor. However, a former English missionary came to be the Administration Superintendent, saving David those technicalities. But the three fellow-missionary nursing sisters from England were indispensable, particularly until David could master the Bengali language.

He should have gone to the language school at Darjeeling for three months but could not leave Sarenga. Jackie had a lot of fun learning the language from their native maid, the cook and the gardener/handyman, but young Paul excelled naturally as he found his pleasure with the lowest cast urchins. Jackie liked their large house, adjoining the hospital, but suffered many long hours without her husband's company. In one letter to me she said: "sometimes we pass each other, by chance". But her down-to-earth attitude and utter devotion kept her smiling.

As time went on David became superintendent of Sarenga hospital and totally responsible of everything, not least the shortage of money to maintain the work. Patients were expected to pay a little for their treatment but their obvious poverty restricted the hospital's appeal. Some patients travelled from miles away, some by ox-cart; in most cases members of the family came and stayed with them, sleeping under beds or in the hospital compound. With the delivery of so many babies came the realization of the importance of Family Planning and, accompanied by Iris, David attended a conference at Delhi on that subject.

Late in 1968, a year and a half after their arrival in India, David's letters revealed both anxiety and pleasure that the work was growing apace. Out-patients had increased to 200 per day and the maternity work had expanded so that a 14-bed ward was crowded with 30 mothers-to-be. David had pursuaded the Calcutta Rotary Club that running water was a necessity and they had sunk a tube-well in the hospital compound for him, a first step to redeem the problem. But the young doctor was not satisfied with only help from 'Rotary' in India, for contacts in Lancashire resulted in £1,000 from Rotary there. He also interested the Bengal Church District Synod in the urgent need of new hospital buildings for his Labour Ward, Sisters' Quarters, Operating Theatre, Laboratory, Dispensary, Ante-natal and Family Planning Clinic and an additional Doctor's House. All they would now have to do would be to plan and discover the cost — then raise the money!

The Indian Government apparently did not realise how important 'Sarenga' was for her people and it was urgently necessary for the small annual grant of money to be drastically increased, and then to rise with the swelling numbers of patients being treated. Funds from the Methodist Missionary Society also needed to rise radically, and David was not slow to tap all these sources. But even in the midst of his busy life and great responsibility, Doctor Goodall could find time for *sport;* he accepted an invitation to represent Calcutta Rugby Football Club in an Indian team to compete against Ceylon. Spending only six days in Colombo, he played in five matches and made useful contacts there and also on his return journey. Stopping at Delhi he attended the *Christian Medical Association of India Conference* as an executive member and Regional Secretary for Bengal and Bihar — "just to ensure that I have enough to do!" he said in his letter.

This active relaxation was made possible by the arrival of two Indian missionary doctors at the hospital, plus the fact that Jackie was being increasingly useful to the nurses.

In 1970, we welcomed Jackie, David, Paul and Mark back at the 'little chapel' for their first home furlough. The Liverpool Methodist Circuit made good use of David for Sundays and week-night meetings where he was able to show slides of both hospital and staff, and enjoin both young and older to support the work by their interest, prayer and money. A fellow local-preacher had died and bequeathed £250 to Sarenga, and David's home church also helped in various ways. Obviously Jackie and the children were very popular, and our people were very supportive in many personal ways. My wife and I welcomed them in a visit to our home and I valued a long walk and talk to David. The Teenagers of Banks Road made a special effort by borrowing an old bed from Broadgreen hospital and pushing it about six miles (bearing a *casualty)* back to the chapel, collecting money on the way.

Returning by air in October 1970, our missionaries were happy to see some of their new building plans completed in the Maternity Village, for in February 1970 *OXFAM* representatives had visited the hospitl and granted the necessary money. Subsequently two OXFAM Regional Organisers had conducted the opening ceremony. Attendances at the ante-natal clinic in 1970 were 3,500 and 766 babies were delivered, but, remembering family planning, over 150 female sterilizations had been performed. There had also been need to increase isolation capacity in the childrens' ward, this need was now met by a new 24-bed ward and at the Thanksgiving Service the eldest boy patient who cut the tape had been a Sarenga baby.

Probably encouraged by Dr. Goodall's wide contacts in the chief cities and towns of India and even Bonn, in Germany, where he visited during his furlough, many people of authority in the medical and missionary world were aroused by the modernizing and development of his hospital. David's letters contain the names of many friends old and new.

The next November was historic for christians in India for *The United Church of North India* was born and David, with some of his staff, was present at the unification ceremony at Calcutta's St. Paul's Cathedral. In the following May the Bishop of the Diocese in the new C.N.I. visited them at Sarenga. Little has been said of the religious life of the hospital and its connection with the local Methodist church. All the christian hospital staff attended morning prayers in the hospital each day and that relationship, according to David, pervaded all their work. The community in their area of North Bengal had confidence in Sarenga hospital, preferring their service before state facilities nearer to their homes. David had not been happy with the local church, telling me that the foundations of the people were fragile and lacking responsibility; undoubtedly judging them by his own dynamic standards.

A very good aspect of the hospital was the continuing expansion of the training of local girls as nurses and the fine quality of the senior nursing staff. In a letter to me of 1978 David referred to the completed Nurses' Hostel and Training School at his hospital and, with understandable pride added, "we have just taken a new class of thirty student nurses".

By now he and his wife had served for more than ten years at Sarenga hospital and they looked forward to a furlough in England in 1979. Now the primitive conditions of 1967 had almost miraculously changed, their premises and conditions could bear comparison with England's smaller hospitals. Hospital staff had increased and now David had four doctor colleagues, an increase of 500% on his early days. But in addition to successes there were continual annual financial running deficits to cause worry and David was not slow to lay the need at the Goverment's door. If the need was not met adequately, David's letter said: "We will have no alternative but to hand over the hospital to the Government". But I am glad to give another quote: "We've still got plenty of problems, but the bold, imaginative approach seems the best!" During their 1979 furlough, his friends at the 'little chapel' could witness at his lectures not only his slides of buildings and people, but David's joy and enthusiasm whilst he attributed his audience as partners in their successes.

That letter of 1978 from David had been his first to me for a few years. I wrote to him monthly and they were always appreciative but David could only spare time when away from 'living over the shop'. Consequently, when Jackie bravely wrote in February 1976 the letter was doubly welcome.

Their third child, Neil, was now a toddler, spending his time with low-cast children and speaking like a native. But now, there was an additional member of the family, a baby girl. During a time when the female ward was understaffed, Jackie gave a hand. A patient with a rare form of cancer had a tiny baby and the nurse prevailed upon Mrs Goodall to care for it during the day. The patient's husband was dead and no one visited her; she, too, died and no relative could be found. Jackie wrote: "I was left holding the baby". She became a treasure to their family and they called her Shona (meaning 'gold' in Bengali). The boys adored her and steps were taken to adopt the baby. (Legal adoption took years to achieve and now she is Shona Goodall, a very bright, active, lovely young lady of whom they are very proud).

The letter, on Indian, christian notepaper, had a novel heading on each of three pages; a logo illustrating an Indian craft with a suitable Bible text. The page describing Shona was entitled: "O Lord . . . we are the clay and Thou our Potter, Isa. 64:8. The other two pages illustrated Psa. 90:17 and Isa. 48:21.

The following year Jackie spent six months in Darjeeling in quarters close to the children's school. In 1980 the needs of the education of their three boys coincided with circumstances that enabled David to return to his hospital appointments in Liverpool. On an earlier furlough in England he had qualified as a consultant and new avenue for his skills and devotion was now opening. As, in England, he prepared for the consultancy, the family resided for a time in a tiny street house 'under-the-bridge' and adjacent to their spiritual home. Then back to the pressures of the Sarenga hospital.

'All work and no play makes Jack a dull boy', the proverb says, and certainly David Goodall was never dull. When, on short vacations, he was able to join his wife in the comparative cool of Darjeeling, he could view the high mountains of the Himalaya's and was attracted to the climbing school of the famous *Tensing*. When he played games he had to be fully extended and the Sarenga staff learned by example how football goalkeeping should be performed. Other snippets from his letters tell of his antics when the monsoon broke after 115° of heat — the Doctor Sahib, clothed and gyrating in the descending torrent. He encouraged the staff to happily and actively use their leisure whilst not neglecting prayertime and expertise. David and Jackie observed the christian festivals even though the Christmas dinner consisted only of egg and chips, and I remember the chagrin of David's father, Arthur, when the table-manners of the home-coming family failed to approximate to English standards.

Now another superintendent had been found for Sarenga hospital and the Goodalls were able on their return to England to raise a mortgage on a larger house in South Liverpool more suitable for a notable consultant doctor. His work in India only warranted the low income that the Methodist Missionary Society could grant to their missionaries. The new affluence, so suitable to our 'enlightened' civilization — and necessary for his large family — served to underline the sacrifices made by missionary persons and workers.

But Sarenga was ever in his mind and circumstances again conspired to enable him to keep in vital touch and occasional visits were made. The Liverpool School of Tropical Medicine, notable historically for its discovery and defeat of the West African scourge of malaria, and of continuing significance, saw David as a 'godsend' with his intimate Asian knowledge and language. In co-operation with their need he visited Delhi and other Indian centres for introducing good training methods for indigenous medical students, whilst also encouraging the staff at Sarenga.

Their christian friends at the 'little chapel' were glad to have the family 'back home' and attending their services. Jackie became especially useful to young families 'Under-the-Bridge' and led a 'toddlers and parents' group whilst David became the Church Secretary. But David's *absences* were accepted as inevitable for in addition to his local preaching in Liverpool churches and lecturing on behalf of the Methodist Missions his presence in a church service or meeting would sometimes be broken by his *bleeper* sounding to order his attendance at a complicated childbirth at the hospital six miles away. He would, however, insist upon maintaining interest in the Church scout group and for a time became Group Scout Leader when his father relinguished the post by reason of ill-health.

Most essentially, Doctor Goodall remained a hospital man; he was devoted to his patients and had a special delight to tend Asian women in Liverpool, surprised at his knowledge of the culture and language. But another Lancashire town whose cotton mills had attracted a substantial population of Indian workers, became interested in David (as indicated earlier in my story) and early in 1985 he was appointed as a consultant in the Blackburn hospital. There, now three years on, we must leave him, still so very busy that his wife Jackie only expexts to see him late at night. He has been back to his spiritual home to preach the Church Anniversary Sermons in May 1988, and he and his family retain 'a very dear connection' with their many friends at church.

Back in the year 1983, whilst on furlough in Liverpool, the writer invited Doctor Goodall to speak to the young men of the *Unemployed Club* who meet in the church hall on one afternoon each week. Those deprived men, several with antagonism to 'the Authorities' showed instant resentment to being 'talked to'. Before glowering faces I introduced David, with great trepidation. Smilingly David addressed them in *scouse.* (I must explain that the working classes in Central Liverpool, with mixed generations of Welsh, Irish and seafarers from the past, have a careless dialect sprinkled with humorous phrases causing such citizens to be called *Scousers).* The young men were taken aback and then were interested as David introduced anecdotes of sport, going on to relate how he had won an *international cap* playing rugby football for India against Ceylon. Soon they were involved with David in his hospital and his patients, brought in by bullock-cart. The writer had to call a halt as Scouse and Pakistani lilted stories held the lads enthralled; they did not want to let him go and even continued the conversations with him out in the street.

In later years, as David was leaving Liverpool for Blackburn, I referred to the broad Lancashire dialect of Blackburn, humorously suggesting to David that he was bound to acquire a third string to his mimicry of primitive Liverpool and Pakistani speech; a unique mixture! On further contemplation, if we ask him to preach the Church Anniversary Sermons again, ten years from now, it will be very interesting. But whatever his speech, grave or gay, I am sure it will continue to reflect that *WORD* sent from heaven to be our Saviour, learned at his parent's knee and in the 'little chapel under-the-bridge'; words of christian commitment and compassion.

Keith Goodall, Chief Ambulance Officer, South Glamorgan Health Authority (wearing the insignia of the President of the Association of Chief Ambulance Officers).

Chapter VI

THE GOODALL FAMILY
(Continued)

Keith Goodall (1945-   )

Whilst David Goodall devotes his life to healing and saving life, and especially to bringing new life safely into the world, his younger brother, Keith, represents the supply line between the community and the hospital; he is an eminent Ambulance Officer.

A Sunday School scholar at the 'little chapel' from infancy, he became a wolf cub as brother David progressed as a scout. Quieter than David, his regular progress was less noticeable but very persistent; he was not such a robust player of games, rather a steady achiever of progressive goals. From 1957 and for seven years he attended the Holt High School and in 1964 joined the Liverpool Ambulance Service as a cadet.

Immediately he seemed to have slotted into a profession that claimed his ardour and devotion for, in less than two years (in June 1966), he was awarded the *Cadet of the Year Trophy* and, becoming an ambulanceman, was promoted as Sub-Officer in September 1969. Not content with progress only in Liverpool he entered, and won, the *National Ambulance Driving Trophy* in July 1969. The following year he cast around for higher promotion and in the December became a *Divisional Ambulance Officer* for the county of Flintshire in Wales.

His boyhood efficiency as a scout patrol leader, and copying brother David's bent on first-aid training with the boys of his patrol, then seemed to blossom for they made him the *Training Officer for the Flintshire Service.* This led to his appointment in January 1974, at the age of 28 years, to be Chief Ambulance Officer of the Powys Health Authority in South Wales; the youngest person ever to be appointed as a 'Chief'.

On the way to these promotions Keith maintained a wide interest in his fellow ambulancemen and in 1966, only two years after joining as a cadet in Liverpool, he was elected a member of the *National Council of the Institute of Certified Ambulance Personnel,* continuing to serve until 1976.

In 1973 he was awarded a *Churchill Fellowship.* The Winston Churchill Memorial Trust enables men and women to travel abroad to widen their knowledge in the field of their own activity. For Keith it meant three months travelling in Norway, Sweden, Finland, Denmark and Germany, studying each of their ambulance services, staff and vehicles. Later, in 1974, in a ceremony in London's Festival Hall, he received his Churchill Fellow's Medallion from H.R.H. The Prince of Wales.

At the age of 21 Keith married, within the 'little chapel', Lynne Weaver. Lynne, a physics teacher, trained in the Didsbury College, Manchester. They set up their home in a new house near Wigan, both travelling into Liverpool each day. Housing in Liverpool, at the right price, was a problem but in just over a year they found residence nearer home and work at Hale, and their first child Andrew was born there in 1969. But promotion to the Flintshire (North Wales) Ambulance Service as Divisional Officer in December 1970 changed their address again to Prestatyn.

Similar to brother David, Keith had trained at Banks Road to be a Local Preacher, and each change of residence quickly brought husband and wife into welcome membership of the local Methodist Church. Their next move was from North to South Wales in January 1974, when he became the Chief Ambulance Officer for Powys, as stated. Making their home in Crickhowell, Powys, they became church members at Abergavenny Methodist Church and from 1976 to 1983 they were members of St. Edmunds (Church of Wales), nearer home at Crickhowell, and at that church Andrew, their eldest child, was 'confirmed' by the Bishop of Swansea. In the Autumn of 1981, little Andrew distinguished himself by touring with the Welsh National Opera as the boy soprano in 'The Magic Flute'. Keith also preached in St. Edmunds on three occasions and from their later Cardiff home, in 1987, the family were invited back to open the church's Christmas Fayre.

Continuing an intimate interest in ambulance staff conditions as he progressed to higher office, Mr Goodall was appointed by the Secretaries of State for Health and Social Services to membership of the National Staff Committee for Ambulance Staff, a position he held from 1978 to 1986. Similarly, the Secretary of State invited him to serve on a working party concerning the *Problems of Long Serving Ambulance Men;* this occurred in 1985. But we are rushing ahead of our story for in April 1983 Keith was appointed Chief Ambulance Officer of the South Glamorgan Health Authority, also with responsibility for managing Health Authority Transport, and Cardiff became his base and home.

Keith and Lynne set up their home, with their three children, in the suburb of Wenvoe, near to the Ambulance Service headquarters for South Glamorgan, and very soon Keith helped to form a Venture Scout Unit and in 1985 he became the Group Scout Leader of all the sections of the 1st Wenvoe Group. It may seem trivial, on taking up an important public position as chief of a force of 160 ambulance workers with 60 ambulances that transport 4,000 patients each week, to engage in *voluntary activities* with teenagers and children. Very likely our subject never thought that he needed a therapy to control his increasing responsibility and speedy rise to very important authority. Those who do place themselves at the disposal of uninhibited youngsters in a caring way soon lose a sense of their own importance and gain natural responses that are a privilege. Before we leave the scouting scene, I must mention the Expedition to Europe of the Venture Scout Unit that Keith led in 1986. They spent time in France, Switzerland and Italy (visiting Rome and Assisi).

The family linked up with the Church of Wales in Wenvoe and at St. Mary's the younger children, Ruth and Jonathan, were confirmed by the Bishop of Llandaff. During the period before and after Keith's promotion to be Chief of South Glamorgan, he organised the *National Conference of the Association of Chief Ambulance Officers* (1980 to 1985) and for the year 1982/3 he was elected *President of the Ambulance Service Institute.* Then for the year 1984/5 he was elected *President of the Association of Chief Ambulance Officers;* the latter presidency gave him the distinction, at the age of 38, of being the youngest ever to receive that honour. Receiving and wearing the chain of office he treasures the miniature replica bestowed and praised his South Glamorgan staff for their 'dedication, professionalism, and loyalty'.

The South Wales Leisure and Entertainment Guide for December 1985 contains Keith's smiling portrait and a profile of his activities; I quote: "Under Keith Goodall's direction, the South Glamorgan ambulance service has changed dramatically, bringing in its wake a new breed of professionalism". Then areas of successful organisation are itemised under headings: *Co-ordination of emergency services; nursing teams, fire protection in hospitals, integration in management structure, a comprehensive communications network* which includes quick, modern alerting of the Barry lifeboat crews. All health service vehicles rationalised down to dispatch bikes, laundry vans and buses for nurses. "Advanced training is now given to ambulance drivers" and details are enumerated to show how lives are saved on the way to hospital.

In March 1986 Keith launched a very interesting monthly magazine for the staff of the South Glamorgan Ambulance Service and in a foreword of the first issue his wide interest in every section of his staff is abundantly apparent: I quote one of his four paragraphs: "Professionalism, qualifications and pay seem synonymous with the new mood in the Service and for those of us with 'Years of Service' behind us, the very satisfactory conclusion of the somewhat protracted pay negotiations, the enhanced status of the Service and the way clear to develop Extended Training seem the fruits of many years of labour".

His editor presents contents of fourteen articles of interest, humour, information and happenings of which any service could be proud. To me it expresses much of the character and drive of their Chief Officer. A happy photograph under the title 'Didn't We Do Well!' shows 25 happy people, in various uniforms and none, posing round the back of an ambulance overflowing with 600 hampers of food and goodies resulting from a *'Fill an Ambulance'* appeal: Keith, crouching as one of them in his shirt sleeves, wears the widest smile of any.

Keith uses the Government *Youth Training Scheme* (Y.T.S.) to the advantage of the Ambulance Service. Taking on groups of twelve young people aged 16-17 he pays them an enhanced weekly wage whilst giving them a thorough training as ambulancemen. He even goes beyond the younger age groups; I have a newspaper article and pictures of Wolf Cubs at the central ambulance station, kitted out with uniform tunics and caps. What romance and realism would be imprinted in mind and imagination; adventure indeed!

I am also privileged to have an 86-page booklet which, in a five-page introduction, Keith Goodall states: "In April 1986 I received an invitation from Dr. Brenildo Tavares, the *Conference Organiser of the World Association of Emergency and Disaster Medicine,* to present a Paper at the 5th World Congress on Emergency and Disaster Medicine which was to be held in Rio in May 1987. The invitation suggested a Paper on the Organization, Training and Operation of the South Glamorgan Ambulance Service". Of course Keith wanted to contribute all he could for such a humanitarian World Scheme but he also had the vision to benefit his own County Organization and particularly the youth of his force thereby. He had an efficient Staff Officer responsible for a developing Cadet Training Scheme; they consulted and contrived a scheme that would involve six of the ambulance cadets, soon to take their Induction Course. They planned to take the six cadets on an expedition to Brazil for 21 days and covering the week of the *Emergency and Disaster Conference.* The first thing was to get the six youths and their parents interested and involved, for jointly they would have to give, or raise, all the cost. The first overture was to test out the lads by a week-end expedition to the Black Mountains in Powys, familiar to Keith with his Venture Scouts. The rigours of a second trip to the Black Mountains confirmed their faith in the cadets' enthusiasm and tenacity.

It was to take nearly twelve months' very intensive preparation and fund-raising to prepare, and the tremendous amount of detailed planning cannot be recounted here. Keith and his Staff Officer had to assume legal guardianship of the six young men. The plan was for full involvement in the *Emergency and Disater Conference* in the first week; close activity with the *Brazilian Red Cross* in the second, and the *Duke of Edinburgh Gold Award Expedition/ Exploration,* finally.

The full story of their 'hare-brained scheme', to use Keith's words, are contained in two volumes of reports of considerable detail. Many problems with people and terrain were met and overcome, each cadet reporting as individuals and collectively. A short epilogue avers that all of the cadets were different persons on their return, and their leaders learned abundantly in a manner that would be fruitful and rewarding for the Service and themselves. Calling their expedition 'Cadex 87 Brazil' a good deal of local publicity resulted and dozens of firms and organisations supported them with equipment whilst the South Glamorgan Authority gave payed leave to all the party. As a biased person I would say it was 'Scouting par excellence', stimulating for youth and healthy for city and public services; I congratulate the boy from the 'little chapel under-the bridge'.

Foreground: Arthur Goodall (father of David, Keith and Colin), as scoutmaster of the 20th Allerton Troop, supervising a bridge-building display. (the writer in the background).

Chapter VII

THE GOODALL FAMILY
(Continued)

Colin Goodall (1953-   )

The Garston factory of Wilson Bros. Bobbin Works employed up to 50% of the 'little chapel' people until it closed down in 1958. The largest factory in the world for the production of shuttles and bobbins for the cotton industry's spinning and weaving mills, had a riverside site under-the-bridge and more than one thousand 'locals' worked there, women and men.

From youth, Colin's father worked there until closure, residing close enough to leave five minutes before 6.00 am buzzer blew each morning. Emigrating on marriage to a home a mile away, their first two sons were free to adopt more adventurous working lives, as already related. But Colin, the youngest, was to experience the 'common to Liverpool' drifting away of industry and shipping employment. Nevertheless, Colin imitated his father by becoming a toolmaker in an engineering works, but remote from Garston. Local primary school led to Toxteth High School in 1964 and in 1969 he became an apprentice toolmaker in an electrical switch-gear factory in North Liverpool.

With all the rest of the family, and from infancy, Colin enjoyed life at the 'little chapel', slipping naturally into a community where numerous people, not of the Goodall family, became quite naturally christian aunts and uncles. Scouting, of course, was a 'must' from the age of eleven years and soon he was useful in training others. The family home moved in the year 1960 about four miles away from the chapel-under-the-bridge and Colin, then aged seven, missed the opportunity of becoming a Wolf Cub in his father's group. After five years in the scout troop he progressed as a Venture Scout to explore adventures similar to those enjoyed by his brothers, David and Keith, who were now well advanced in their careers far from the home chapel and older than himself by thirteen and eight years, respectively.

Meanwhile, he became a helper in the church Youth Club and also a Sunday School teacher, thus emulating his father and mother, also Keith and David. (David was now a medical missionary in India).

From childhood he had been a keen member of the Methodist Junior Missionary Association collecting weekly from the Goodall's wide family and also those aunties and uncles of the church already mentioned. The J.M.A. and missionary support in general were to be a continuing passion with him.

Though he remained a member of the 'little chapel' until 1974, soon his distant home and teenage activities curtailed his scouting and he needed working experience. Taking up an apprenticeship at the age of 16 just happened, for it was not easy to find a job of your choice. But an apprenticeship in an interesting employment, using one's hands and brain along with other young men, was rather like an extension of his scouting experiences.

His elder brothers had studied hard for their medical and ambulance careers, and Colin took City and Guilds courses at the two Technical Colleges of Old Swan and West Derby, both of North Liverpool. In the course of his travel in that area he met Susan at Formby railway station in 1972, and friendship ripened to a wedding in June 1977 at Banks Road Chapel. On their first meeting Susan was attending a teacher training college but their interests were similar, and, as a Guide specializing in Brownie training, she and Colin were to form a useful partnership in future years.

After five years' apprenticeship, Colin secured a place in Worcester as a toolmaker in a metal castings firm, and continued study at the City Technical College for the Higher National Certificate. Also for the year 1974/5 he attended the local Methodist church. In 1975 he improved his prospects as a toolmaker with an engineering firm at Walsall, and for two years studied at the Birmingham Polytechnic three evenings per week to complete his Higher National Certificate.

Naturally, he had hardly settled in his new house in the suburb of Streetly before scouting again claimed his energies. The Group Scout Leader of the 2nd Streetly, a group 260-strong, found Colin to be a heaven-sent benefit. A normal scout group is fortunate to have full ranks of three units; cub pack, a scout troop and a venture group, each not to exceed a recommended maximum of 36, 40 and 12 respectively. But the 2nd Streetly was the largest group in the Birmingham area, which includes Walsall. The G.S.L.'s headache was for responsible, trained officers; he had three cub packs, two troops and a large venture group of 40, but one cub pack had no Akela and to comply with regulations that pack must close down and adversely affect the intake of boys into the group.

Colin Goodall training Cub-Scout Sixers.

Colin, along with his wife Sue, were the ideal solution, for an Akela of worth contributes a lot of time and considerable homelife for thirty-six little rascals under their care. Being an 'open' group, not connected to a church or similar organisation, our young couple experienced fellow scouters less devoted to their young charges than in Colin's home scout group. Yet it was satisfactory to work in a very large group with good financial support from parents and various interested parties.

In the course of time they found two or three kindred christian helpers and also were welcomed at the homes of the boys. As Sue also had linked up as a Brownie Guider with girls of the same families happy relationships resulted and also Colin became cook and helper at brownie camps and outings with the positions reversed on cub occasions. Colin remained Akela for twelve years, contributing considerably to the prosperity of the 2nd Streetly Scout Group.

Meanwhile, their first connection on moving to Walsall in 1975 was to become members at the Anchor Road Methodist Church, in Aldridge, near to their temporary home. Moving house in 1977 they again attended the nearest Methodist church at Blackwood Road in Streetly, and among various church commitments Colin became the

Youth Fellowship Leader. At last Colin and Sue were able to attain their own house in 1979 but it was five miles away from their church in Streetly; still they gladly, but inconveniently, maintained their church membership with its obligations. Becoming friendly with new neighbours who attended the local C. of E. St. Thomas's Church, they consented to visit the church nearby and were pleased with the friendly atmosphere and lively services.

Colin told me of his trepidition to venture away from his familiar Methodist connections and forms of service into the formalism of the Anglican Prayer Book but, together with his wife, they decided on a fair trial of new experiences. Very soon they made wider christian friendships and enjoyed a welcoming people to the extent of joining them in responsibilities and tasks similar to their normal Methodist involvement. Undoubtedly, Colin's early training and service at the '*little-chapel-under-the-bridge*' and his family traditions contributed to his adaptability for in a very short time he became a Sides Person, a Steward, a member of the Church Council, and the Chairman of the Missionary Committee, etc.

Among the etceteras was a lively interest in the Church Musical Ministry Team (Colin is a pianist) which overflowed into an active participation with the *Roger Jones Religious Musicals* as they tour many of our cities and towns. They took part in the popular '*Star Gazers*' in 1983, '*Saints Alive*' in 1984, '*Greater than Gold*' in 1985 and went on tour with the main Birmingham Choir in '*From Pharoah to Freedom*' in 1985/86, and '*While Shepherds Watched*' in 1987/88.

As the Chairman of the Missionary Committee, Colin was pursuing and developing his childhood interest when he was a juvenile collector for Overseas Missions and, of course, his brother David was the Superintendent of the Methodist Mission hospital in Sarenga, West Bengal, India. At St. Thomas's a scheme has developed where missionaries and their families are adopted by responsible people who correspond and generate help and finance. Colin and Sue support one such family in Ghana (name given), one of six missionary families supported by the church and in Colin's realm of responsibility. That responsibility is both wearing and often frustrating, according to Colin, for it is very hard to motivate people, obsessed with the problems of life in town and church, to adequately support those sincere christians who give themselves to serve Christ and their fellows in distant places.

Colin confesses that his new-found activities with and for his new church were amply rewarded by his additional friendships and he was soon to experience loving support in a crisis situation. He and

Sue were now comfortably settled in their very own home, for which they had worked hard, and they were able now to consider starting a family. To their delight Rebekah was born in February 1983, healthy and bonny. Released from hospital on the second day, all was going well but on the seventh day they had a little anxiety and called their doctor. For health checks Rebekah returned to hospital on the eighth day but on the ninth day she died from an unusual heart condition. The young couple were devastated, their high hopes for a little girl had been granted, and, for but a week, their joy had been unbounded. In deep sorrow they found comfort only in their faith and in the sympathy and support of their new church which now, five years later, Colin speaks of most thankfully. As the months of cold sorrow drifted on they found a growing warmth toward others with family sorrows and, to date, they have developed a ministry to those in the church who need an understanding friendship at their crisis-time.

The next year they were blessed with the birth of Matthew and in 1987 Philip was born, but Colin (writing to me) still holds Rebekah very dear in his heart. Their two boys are extra precious to them and for a time Colin has passed on his position of Akela to another as their programme of activities, particularly in the church, has expanded; but he suspects that as Matthew and Philip reach cub and scout age, scouting in the blood may assume a priority again. He is proud of his family and his own expertise in scouting and youth work and happily boasts of his high scouting honours of the *Wood Badge* and the *Gilwell Scarf,* presented to him during 1979. However, being busy in church and scout work must remain secondary to Colin's industrial life. Indeed, his employers increasingly recognise his qualities in the training of new entrants; somewhat akin to his voluntary skills with Venture Scouts. Additonally he has now become the Works Safety Officer.

Very occasionally Colin finds time to visit the 'little chapel' with his parents for the mutual pleasure of friends of long-ago and early scout days. Recently I learned of a quaint link that Colin retains. A prized family scouting relic is his father's old, wide-brim scout hat, as favoured by Baden-Powell until it was changed to the beret at about the time of Colin's birth. It will now be specially precious for since the writer's enquiries and the ready co-operation of Colin, his father died at the age of 73.

Both his father and mother had failing health in recent years, giving anxiety to each of the three brothers and much professional attention from the eldest, Doctor David, who frequently visited them from his very busy headquarters at the Blackburn hospital over sixty miles away. Their mother, Elsie, regained her health considerably as their father, Arthur, suffered his final illness. I spoke to her on the day of Arthur's funeral, she was calm and strong, thankful to have all the family around her. The three sons, and Joan, living in four towns widespread in England and Wales wished her to come to their homes but she continued to live alone in the family house. Eight weeks later we were all summoned to *her* funeral.

Both funerals were solemn, memorable events in the lives of the members of the 'little-chapel-under-the-bridge' and our own minister was well aware of the considerable service in church and scouts of Arthur and the devoted motherhood of Elsie. The symbolism of the scout tracking sign was used at Arthur's service: a circle of pebbles with a centre stone to denote: *I have gone home!* was set out near the coffin.

So the story of the youngest of my ten remarkable men is told of Colin Goodall although he has not specialised in a career of outstanding importance. As a member of the Goodall family and a product of the 'little chapel' he can be noted as an ordinary person leading a typical working life to a very high standard as a christian. He, along with Susan, has met life's needs as they have presented themselves in a dedicated fashion, which reminds me of a line in Henry M. Butler's hymn: 'Lift up your hearts! We lift them, Lord, to thee': The line is: *'Low lies the best till lifted up to heaven'*. In such circumstances *the ordinary* becomes *extraordinary.*

Harry Smith: artist, writer and editor. In 1985 reading his first edition of 'R.E. Today' (religious education term magazine) of which he is the initiator and editor.

Chapter VIII

Harry Smith (1939-   )

As I am privileged to write about ten men, all influenced by the same 'little-chapel-under-the-bridge', I must consider, a little more intimately, the blend of Divine Resources acting upon my characters. An obvious common denominator was that all served in the same Scout Group during impressionable childhood. If I were writing about that scout group or comparing it with other Liverpool groups, I could not make out a spectacular case, rather the reverse, for wealth and good educational standards and numbers of boys could not weigh in our favour. Nor would the fact that these boys were *scouts* be vital if divorced from the more important factors of christian training and example through the church and its ministers. Then, of primary importance, of course, were the parents, homes and families of our favoured characters.

All three groups were a happy blend in the influence of the 'little chapel' and none more so than evidenced by our ninth character, HARRY SMITH.

A book could be written about the unique Smith Family, and, still more interestingly, about young children in general, for indeed, to coin an oft-repeated phrase: 'The child is father of the man'. Jesus truly put that fact in worthy perspective when he rebuked his disciples (as the Good News Bible records) "Let the children come to me and do not stop them, because the Kingdom of Heaven belongs to such as these". The old Bible reference (of 1611) "Suffer the little children to come unto me", often confused the simple in my younger days, and I remember an argument I had with a man who could not believe in Jesus because he made children suffer and die so that they could be with him on the other side of the divide — "Gross poppycock!" But I can recollect my own, and common feeling in the days when infant diseases killed many children.

In my early 20's (year 1931) I left the 'little chapel' for six years, my job transferred to another town, but maintaining my interest and occasional visits. Among the good friends I made, in fresh surroundings, was a bright boy aged eight. Suddenly he died, a victim of diphtheria; his parents were devastated. With the small bunch of flowers I laid on the coffin my label included the first two lines of a children's hymn, not now used in our churches:

'Around the throne of God in heaven,
Thousands of children stand'

the verse continued:

'Children whose sins are all forgiven,
A holy, happy band,
Singing, Glory, glory, glory!'

The contrasting point I wish to make concerning our ten prominent people is that in childhood they were called by Jesus to become members of the Kingdom of Heaven, *active in the world* and equipped to go 'Over the Top' in that select army. now I can tell you how I first noticed HARRY SMITH.

He was a wolf cub and I did not particularly notice him among the eighty members of our scout group until the day before the Church's annual Christmas Fair. One of my sons, handy with coloured chalks, had made advertising posters to save overhead expenses. Numerous stalls had been set up in our large school hall and, as we worked to prepare for the fair, little Harry came to me. "Could I let him make some posters?"

He was not in cub uniform and I did not even recognise him as a cub. He was in street uniform — a typical urchin with stockings at half-mast, questionable cleanliness and non-descript clothing. Of course this mite could not make posters but his keen eyes could not bear a refusal, so I took him around the stalls and asked the ladies if he could make small posters for their stalls. We allow a further eighteen months to go by and find young Harry competing in the Methodist Circuit mini-eisteddfod and taking the first prize in his age group, for his imaginative picture. Jump on a further few years and we find him at the drawing table of the London office of the Billy Graham Evangelistic Association publications as the art editor, not only a keen and competent artist but devoted to commending his Lord to others.

What of Harry Smith's family background? I have said that a book could be written about its members; perhaps a little can be written to illustrate the 'little chapel's' influence on the family. All the members of the large family of ALF and MARTHA SMITH had notable and varied characteristics, five girls and three boys, Harry being the youngest boy. the children were born in poverty close to the slum dwelling of Jack Jones's childhood and father Alf was referred to in my chapter on the great trade union leader. Alf never seemed to have a stable job until the 1939/45 war and in the twenty years before his retirement he held the humble job of cleaner in a bus depot. I shared some of his confidences for, in the dozen years before his death in 1984, we had walked many of the fell paths in Cumbria's Lake District together. He had not always been a chapel man. He attributed his gradual conversion to strong christian principles from a kindly act of humbler christians welcoming him to a fireside during bitter weather and bitter poverty. Add to this circumstance also the devotion of a good wife and that, successfully, his large family of children attended the Sunday School at the 'little chapel'. I think my first knowledge of him was when he helped individual scouts from our troop to pass their 'cyclist prificiency' badge by his instruction.

Alf became a powerful christian and a great asset to his church, but a more retiring person was his wife, happily still with us, now quite old. Whilst Alf was a little unpredictable and prone to sudden action as he saw a need arise, Martha was peaceful and reliable; the slender pivot around which the family revolved. People were deceived by Martha's still presence until, perhaps, she would tell of an episode in the family's life with brief wit and humour. Though all but one of her loving brood live far away they keep in close touch, with ever a welcome in their house. I know a little of the varied qualities of the daughters, but, at present, am only relating of the male members of the family who featured in our scout group.

Tom, the eldest, a school master, was an apprentice-served electrician until he felt a dual call to be a local preacher in the Methodist Church and especially involved with 'young people'. Of sound worth in the church and circuit and with a wife of equal devotion, they retain for the home church some of the expertise which other members of the family have taken elsewhere. Tom teaches in a Church of England junior school whilst his wife teaches in the County Primary school adjacent to the 'little chapel', and where Harry, myself, and nearly all the persons mentioned in these pages were educated in their early years. Now, as we turn to our principal, Harry, we will see a relationship in the matters of christian training that further illustrates the diversity in the Smith family and of the christian characters in this book.

Fortunately, although Harry lives and works in Exeter, a couple of hundred miles from Liverpool, he has responded most generously to my request for information on his life and work. I am grateful to be able to quote extensively from his typescript, so factual and full of the adventure of new horizons. I am only sorry that being concise and factual much of his sunny, virile disposition and, no doubt, varied daily adventures must be left to the imagination of those who know him. I started to tell of my first impressions of him, let Harry continue:

"I had my first experience of publishers at the age of 11 when I was paid for drawings which appeared in two Saturday editions of the '*Liverpool Echo*' children's page. My enthusiastic art teacher at Heath Road Secondary School, who gave up his Saturdays to take pupils sketching, persuaded me to take the entrance examination for Liverpool Secondary School of Art.

"A few years later, in my first term at the West of England College of Art (Bristol), a missionary who had been invited to speak at a lunch-time students' meeting, suggested that the Church needed artists and graphic designers who could produce attractive Christian material to compete with secular books, magazines and advertisements. I realised that this was exactly what I wanted to do. The presentation of Christian publications had always depressed me. From that day, I made sure that whenever the opportunity presented itself, the work I produced at College (designs for posters, leaflets, book jackets and record sleeves) would be on a religious theme. My aim was to build up a folder of work which I could present to church agencies when the time came for me to look for a job after graduation".

So, in a few sentences we learn not only of his further education at Heath Road Secondary school, two miles from his home 'under-the-bridge', and of the Liverpool Art School, but we are plunged quickly into his life-style, beliefs and hopes. But previously at the 'little chapel', its Sunday School, clubs, scouts and services, he was maturing within his family, not claiming the bright light of sudden christian revelation — growing, as many of us did. In a telephone conversation with me, he highlighted the *general* rather than the particular influences of the 'little chapel' and referred to the constancy of certain people, even saying that I, myself, was not adverse to rushing straight from daily and nightly work to keep faith with his young contemporaries.

How were his dreams encouraged now that he was launched in life?

"With the enthusiasm of youth, I had not considered that most church agencies would not be interested in employing me! Unlike today, when agents like the Salvation Army, Christian Aid and the main Christian publishers employ professional designers, illustrators and lay-out artists, I doubt if there were more than half a dozen professional artists in the UK producing work for Christian institutions. Time after time I was greeted with blank expressions from leaders of religious societies who published material which would have found difficulty competing with the exhilerating design of the telephone directory! But they could not imagine why they might need a professional graphic designer.

"Fortunately, I came across 'Crusade' magazine. The Editor, David Winter (now head of Religious Broadcasting for BBC Radio) and the Art Director, Gordon Stowell, pointed me in the direction of the Billy Graham Evangelistic Association.

"As usual, the Americans were about ten years ahead of the UK. The editor of *'The Christian Newspaper',* which Billy Graham had recently taken over (it had been in existence since the Moody and Sankey revival of 1865, and looked like it!), seemed delighted to meet me. "I've just been advised by our Minniapolis office that it's time we appointed a full-time Art Editor", she said. Could this be divine intervention! Within months we had launched a new-style *"Christian Newspaper".* A few years later I felt very proud to initiate the first Church newspaper with coloured pictures using the latest photo-litho printing method — until I discovered that the Roman Catholic newspaper, *"The Universe",* had pipped me to the post a week before! (Don't believe that there isn't healthy competition within the Christian press — it's what keeps the journalists' inky adrenalin flowing!) My wife, Diana (also an artist) produced the childrens' page of the newspaper with me. In those days I was not only designing the newspaper and building up its photo library, I also had the opportunity to report on youth events around the country and, on one occasion, I visited Amsterdam to report Cliff Richard's first charity tour. By now (1966-68), the Christian publishing world was waking up to the need for attractive publications and publicity and there was a sudden interest in the production of locally produced ecumenical newspapers. The British Council of Churches invited me to speak at a national conference to encourage more towns and cities to think more seriously about well-produced inter-church newspapers".

Harry married Diana in 1964, a joining of kindred souls, I would say, for both were artists with a passion for christian enlightenment. Most of Harry's future production of christian literature bore Diana's name also, as leading some phase of the production, and she seemed to fit in well with the unique Smith family. Harry's saga with the Graham newspaper etc. led him to recount an earlier experience. he told me how he had been influenced at a mission campaign run at the 'little chapel' by a team of Methodist theological students from the Manchester Hartley-Victoria College. he commented that some of the students had become committed christians after attending Billy Graham evangelical meetings and Harry drew the connection with his own subsequent work with Billy Graham. I, too, remember a connection of Harry with our local evangelical campaign; but a humorous one.

Harry was now a virile man, oozing good health and sporting a fine beard. A pleasant young women, who was a member of the mission team and a student deaconess, was conducting a friendly meeting of about 60 persons in our church hall. Smilingly she referred to bearded men and said she had never been kissed by one, when there was a rumpus from the rear of the hall and Harry advanced, arms outstretched, like a menacing gorilla. A fluttering escape run, in limited space, only delayed for a moment Harry's strong embrace and the imprint of his salutation. Regardless of whether delight attended the protagonists, the congregation certainly enjoyed it.

Typically Harry's record continues:

"I thoroughly enjoyed those years rushing around Fleet Street but, in 1968 (after running voluntary youth clubs for a couple of years) I decided to leave journalism and the drawing board and I entered the teaching profession.

"My experience in journalism and my various responsibility posts as a teacher (first in Art, then Music, and finally English Language) proved to be a great advantage ten years later when Heinemann, the educational publishers, commissioned me to write a school assembly book. At that time most assembly books seemed to assume that all children were committed members of the Christian Church and the suggestions for assembly often had no relationship with the creative activities going on in the classrooms. The commission to write the book coincided with a full-time course on Religious Education which I was attending in multicultural Birmingham. During that period I was overwhelmed by the commitment which many Hindus, Muslims and Sikhs had for their faith. It was clearly central to their lives and it disturbed me that assemblies in some schools, where 90% of the children were Muslim, appeared to ignore their faith and culture. I had decided, even before I arrived in Birmingham, that modern British schools require assembly books which expressed the vibrancy and richness of our growing multifaith society. Apart from contributing to multicultural education in a general sense, it is my view that a multifaith approach to religious education and school assembly can challenge, inform and invigorate those who already have a firm faith commitment. Christians have a lot to learn from Muslims; Hindus can learn from the experience of Sikhs and Jews . . . having met children and parents from various faith communities, I decided to go further than my original intention in writing the book; working with people in each religious group, I produced a 'model' assembly designed specifically for the children in each of the major religions. I hoped that headteachers in multifaith schools might show the assembly scripts to parents in the different faith communities and encourage them to work together (perhaps once a month) on assemblies which would meet the specific religious needs of their own children.

"I appreciate that some people feel that this process could cause division in schools, but I am convinced that we cannot reflect the true identity of a school community if we refuse to allow large groups in that community to express the values which are central to their whole way of life. This is possibly one of the most controversial areas within the school curriculum, but if there is a genuine caring concern between staff, parents and children from the moment each new child arrives in the school, seeds of understanding and co-operation can be sown and differences of religious belief can be expressed and acknowledgement without causing dissention. There is a 'conscience clause' in the Education Act which allows parents to withdraw children from religious acts of worship so that no parent needs to feel that his/her child is being 'indoctrinated' into a faith-commitment; on the other hand, some parents may *want* their children to attend a specific act of worship either to strengthen the faith-commitment of the family or to allow the children to observe and learn from the religious worship of others. It is my conviction that the majority of assemblies in a school unite the common values of the school (including a respect for the religious beliefs, festivals, prayers and practices of others and also a respect for those who do not hold any specific religious beliefs). But there is also a place for an occasional assembly arranged specifically for each religious group in the school — supervised by the headteacher and a local religious leader. This assembly should assist in developing the kind of personal dignity and a respect for others which we all need to learn if we are to live together in harmony".

In that long quote I feel sure that many progressive christians will admire the depth and breadth of his statements, along with the urgency to effect wise changes. I note typicality of Harry's character in many of the words and phrases he uses like: 'that modern British schools require assembly books which expressed the vibrancy and richness of our multifaith society'; 'a multifaith approach to religious education and school assembly can challenge, inform and invigorate those who already have a firm faith commitment'; 'a genuine caring concern between staff, parents and children from the moment each new child arrives in the school'; and his closing sentence about 'personal dignity and respect for others'. Such expressions and progressive thinking may owe more to Harry's upbringing in poverty, the love within his large family, and the concepts of Jesus as learned in the 'little chapel', rather than to privileged scholarship.

Harry's final quote carries us on to the year 1988 with considerable admiration for his progress:

"My book, 'Assemblies: A Resource Book for Primary and Middle Schools' was published in 1981 and, to my surprise, two more multifaith assembly books were published by other authors in the same year though neither of them provided acts of worship for particular religious groups.

"In 1979, as my assembly book was being prepared for publication, I became a schools' adviser in Religious Education and Regional Secretary to the Christian Education Movement in the southwest of England. Within months I was invited to lecture on multifaith assemblies at London University, Birmingham University and many other educational centres in England.

"In 1985 my journalist's blood began throbbing again. Having complained for years that there was no magazine produced in a popular and colourful style for teachers of Religious Education, I was given twelve months to re-launch (and edit) 'RE Today' magazine. I gathered together a team of enthusiastic teachers and lecturers to work with me. CEM, the publishers, were nervous about the enormous costs involved in producing a coloured multifaith magazine ('but the cover will cost over £1,000 for each edition!') but, when advertising revenue began to pour in and circulation rose by over 7,000 in two years, the Christian proprietors accepted that professionalism pays off.

"By 1987 I had come full circle. Billy Graham had given me the opportunity to link professionalism with religious commitment; Birmingham expanded my concept of religious commitment and professionalism in the teaching of religion, using the music, dance, drama, art and literary skills which I had developed over the years. God's world is far more wonderful and mysterious than I shall ever know . . . I frequently feel frustrated and appalled by the way religiously committed people treat each other but I still manage to enjoy the journey".

Harry and Diana will be celebrating their Silver Wedding this year (1989). May they continue for a long time to enjoy their journey as God's wonderful and mysterious world continues to give successive dawns of enlightenment.

Fred Green: early leader and 'great encourager' of characters in 'Over the Top'.

Chapter IX

Fred George Green (1900-   )

I once won a prize of a three-penny-silver-'bit' for learning a portion of scripture. The tiny silver coin went out of circulation in about the 1950's, an irritating tiny thing, but treasured beyond my weekly pocket-money in the year 1916. Church collections in the 'little chapel' at the time were usually of copper coins; where some special occasion occurred, perhaps including a cup of tea, a 'silver collection' was declared and it was an extra bounty if a few sixpences, or even a shilling lay in the box among the grist of the tiny silver coins.

My seventeen-year-old Sunday school teacher had risked his own poverty for a few days, by issuing a challenge to his ten nine-year-old boys: "Learn the 23rd Psalm by next Sunday and the best will get 3d" (called 3d then). I ensured his kindly poverty by becoming word-perfect. No balance sheet recorded how recklessly I spent the money, but I still *remember* the psalm throught the succeeding seventy years — treasure indeed! The unlucky teacher was Fred Green; I got to know him better in the following year when he started the 135th Liverpool Troop of boy scouts.

Though, by age, Fred should be first in my stories of *ten* remarkable men, I complete my list with his life because he had great influence on the early lives of the others at first-hand, or second-hand in the case of some. The hymn lines of Charles Wesley seem to be appropriate here: "See how great a flame aspires, kindled by a spark of grace!" for Fred's conversion to Christ happened in this way. As an eleven-year-old, sitting near the back of the 'little chapel' among the congregation during a Sunday evening service, he heard an appeal from Pastor Walter Mawer for people to declare and give their hearts to the Lord Jesus.

It was November 5th 1911, Guy Fawkes Night, and Fred, with the others in the service, could hear the hubbub of celebration; fireworks exploding, rockets, ships' hooters at the docks and railway whistles all making their usual din. Hearing the sincere appeal of the pastor, little Fred stood up, his figure slight and frail. I have no evidence that others stood up; I think not for the pastor made a comment: "and a little child shall lead them!"

From whence came my information? I had never heard of a Pastor Walter Mawer! Fred Green, now at the age of 88 and living in a little

Essex village about 200 miles from Liverpool, has not seen me for nearly 20 years, though he has written on rare occasions. Recently my written appeals to him for some information were fruitless until I had the surprise of receiving a cassette of his voice. Knowing him well during the years from 1917 to 1938, my general knowledge was adequate. The cassette recording was hardly adequate in detail and in modest understatement, but I was grateful for his conversion story which continues: Young Fred ran quickly home as the service closed. Mr Mawer sent someone after him and brought him back. Fred's old voice told of an intimate conversation with the pastor. "We stood by the choir seats", he said, and remembers gratefully the earnest invitation to discipleship.

Fred Green lived in Stanley Street, next-door-but-one from Dan Oakes (the New Guinea missionary) who was six years his junior. Dan was much influenced by him from the year 1918 and about 1926 they both became Methodist Local Preachers together. Fred was born in February 1900 and, unlike most 'under-the-bridge' children, was educated a mile away at a Wesleyan Primary school. Grateful for deeply religious parents he, and his younger sister, loved the Sunday School at the 'little chapel'.

Much of the community social life centred round the church and school. Their own brass band led their popular processions to *'treats'* and *'May Queen'* sports, whilst a 'mutual improvement class' (M.I.C.) supplemented ordinary education for adults with a little schooling, in addition to religious classes and public concerts. Perhaps our eleven-year-old's brave witness in church could be qualified by the fact that he had become a boy-soloist, rehearsed by his elders to sing hymn verses at services and sometimes at concerts. Certainly as I knew him from 1917 he was never too shy to step forward, take initiatives and leadership roles. Chapter II tells how with Bill and Syd, he started the scout troop in 1917; Syd was, of course, Sidney Constable and Bill was Mr Bailey, a church leader and teacher. I suspect that Fred's was the initiative for the venture, using the two Constable brothers (in Sea Scout uniform) to encourage Bill (an ordinary worker in the railway wagon shop) to start the venture.

But Fred Green's cassette account does not minimize the influence of Bill Bailey for, as a child, he remembers Bill teaching him the Junior Church Catechism (quote): "What is man's first aim?" (answer) "To glorify God and enjoy Him for ever!" I also remember Mr Bailey well and one of his interventions is worthy of recollection as germain to our story.

About twenty lads, teenagers and mostly scouts, habitually attended evening church service. During the week and on Sunday afternoons they were in the habit of entering the church via the rear schoolroom and through the door by the pulpit. Unfortunately for a Mr Griffiths, venerable, aged and authoritarian, seated in his regular pew at the front of the transept, where the lads sat together behind him in the evening, the crowd of teenagers clattering in after he was seated, disturbed his reverent demean. One evening Mr Griffiths waited for us in the schoolroom and as our tribe marched in, he roundly condemned our behaviour, demanding that we should face about and come into the church by the main door. We resented this and an altercation was occurring as Bill Bailey walked in. He should have been subservient to the senior official; we warmed to him as he took our part. "Look here, Mr Griffiths, we want these lads in; if necessary I'll take the slates off the roof so they can come to our Lord!" (thus a reference to the gospel incident where friends lowered their sick mate to the feet of Jesus, via the roof).

Older brothers and sisters of the church sometimes conflicted with the teenage Fred Green when he tried to introduce 'modern' ideas into the school or church practices. He tried to alter the Sunday School pattern of the 'big school' where a leader in a large department 'ruled' from the front with little regard for the needs of individuals and age differences. Recommending a change to the *'graded school system'* he gained the enthusiasm of the young and when the change was made, with Fred as superintendent, a number of traditionalists left the church. Thus, posts of varying responsibility in church and school were vacated, having the effect of forcing the young to take responsibilities in a challenging fashion. Fred was always assured of male participation from Scout sources, etc., and girls were not averse to join the adventures.

The under-the-bridge community chiefly earned their bread in local works or dockside. Fred's father worked at the copperworks but Fred had found employment 'in the city' and had a desk job with an important shipping company. His tuppenny tramride into Liverpool each day, widened his friendships and gave him access to books and business practices that stimulated his life-style. Many of us, and particularly enthusiasts like Dan Oakes, were encouraged by Fred to read books and discuss religion as a normality. As we walked about in groups of friends, usually scouts, we had a natural pleasure that was usually Christ-centred.

A great rallying ground was the Wesley Guild because it involved so many young people; Fred was central in its activities. The five sections: *Christian Service, Literary, Devotional, Social* and *Look-*

Out needed five chairmen and five secretaries, plus four or five members on each committee; the President (often Fred) and the treasurer made sure the the *Look-Out* committee brought new members in regularly. Fred Green also became the General Secretary of the Liverpool District Wesley Guild with its 20,000 members, and had friendships with eminent people like the Rev. Dr. W. E. Sangster and Rev. George Allen, the national secretary.

One evening Fred arrived at church sporting in his lapel a new badge. Having only a round circle on it we all queried its meaning; he would not tell us. Later, as our curiosity matured, he allowed us to know that it was a *Regnal Circle* badge and within weeks we had a flourishing Regnal Circle (for men); soon a Women's Circle was started and for many years both circles thrived and friendships with other circles and individuals resulted. The idea was *a circle of friendship* not restricted to christians; one could graduate to the 'inner circle', which implied christian discipleship, without prejudice to the 'outer circle'. Started by the Rev. Donald Standfast among soldiers in the 1914-18 war, it gained thousands of members. Fred Green became the Regnal Vice-President. The Regnal Circle continued at Banks Road until about 1968; for the last dozen-or-so years Arthur Goodall was the Steward (leader), the father of Dr. David Goodall and his brothers.

Returning to the war years, Fred Green was called up to the army in 1918 and became a Corporal; returning in 1919, he resumed as Scoutmaster but his aptitude to take on duties within and beyond the church took him from active scouting by about 1926. This aptitude to take up jobs and lay down others was criticised, but in retrospect can be seen as forcing younger persons to take responsibilities and, in the title of the book, to go *'Over the Top'* as the challenge came. Whilst visiting relatives at Burton-on-Trent in the year 1920, he visited the Wesleyan Sunday School (always snooping for ideas). His 'snooping' succeeded for he saw a lovely girl, Violet Bamford; they fell in love and subsequently married at Burton. Home with him at Garston, she took her place at the 'little chapel' and became invaluable in the Sunday school and church.

Meanwhile, Liverpool Shipping Lines were facing challenges from the southern ports, like Southampton, and Fred had to divert to the expanding steel industry for employment. In 1938 he left Liverpool for London intent upon becoming a business secretary. He joined the staff at St. John's Square, Piccadilly, and remained there for thirty years. He gained the degree of Fellow of the Chartered Institute of Secretaries (F.C.I.S.) and became secretary to some of the household names in the Steel Industry. Once I visited Fred and his wife in their nice home in Stanmore but, whilst I continued to send the monthly newsletter to them, I was not privy to details of the many interesting happenings of Fred's London life.

I know that he took up with his local Methodist church and continued as a sincere and acceptable local preacher. Becoming interested in the USA-based world religious movement, *The Unity Movement,* he eventually became the British Vice-President, holding the office for seven years. On retiring from the city, they made their home in a small village near to Saffron Walden, Essex, and Fred's preaching took him to many villages and churches of all denominations, except Catholics. It was only in 1987 that he retired from preaching at the age of nearly 88 and after 62 years of that important christian mission. Fred never drove a car and he walked many miles on Sundays. His village, with only a small shop, relied on people like Fred to bring back their small needs as he travelled; frequently he visited London. Familywise, Fred and Vi enjoyed visits with their three children, two boys and a girl, who have blessed Fred and Vi with seven grandchildren and two great-grandchildren. In 1985 Violet died, quite suddenly; a great loss to Fred but he continued to live in his village home, alone. I sometimes wish that I could have heard his sermons in the country chapels *after* he had lost his dear wife.

Thinking of my stories of men who had been influenced by Fred in their early days, I wrote a short article recently for our Liverpool Circuit of Methodist Churches under the title *'Stable Results'*. Very briefly I referred to this book and its ten remarkable men originating from our small chapel, I wrote from the angle of my good fortune in *backing winners.* Agreeing that other churches also could claim many *winners,* I made the point that my stories start from the lowly point of an eleven-year-old's conversion and the Pastor's observation: "And a little child shall lead them!"

Undoubtedly my heroes were influenced by others in the church, additional to Fred Green's unique contribution, but *most certainly* the *child of Bethlehem* was the *spark of grace* that caught their imagination and the life, courage and triumph of the *Saviour of the World* was the inspiration of ordinary lads from the *little chapel-under-the-bridge* to venture *over the top.*

Frank Mason – the writer, receiving from the Lord Lieutenant of Merseyside, the award of the Chief Constable of Merseyside for 'Citizen of the Year 1983 (for services in the 'little chapel' for the unemployed).

Chapter X

The Writer, FRANK MASON (1907-   )

Like fresh-air which is wholesome and necessary to healthy life, the *common christian* may be praiseworthy but hardly print-worthy. But the writer who has been a privileged witness of the development and growth of the more effective kind of christian men, particularly when their growth occurred almost together in a common field, such as the little Garston chapel-under-the-bridge, may be permitted to explain the spadework and fertilization in which he had a part.

My recollections of tender childhood are precious, for memory does not extend beyond a certain point of capability. If we do not treasure small incidents that have emerged through the clouds of infant ignorance and innocence, they lose their significance and are lost in the general trivialities of later life. But they are precious.

In the introduction to my book I refer to my earliest conception of the little chapel schoolroom as vast and alien to my tender consciousness. It must have been a little later, when I was a full five years old, that I remember only one incident of my first day at the Council school. It was an incident of guilt; what, at five years old!

At the time my aunt had visited our family and promised *me* a small packet of chocolate if I was a good boy on my first day in school. I had never had such a desirable gift before and when I returned from school I accepted the chocolates with joy; and told a lie. I knew I had *not* been a good boy for I had cried and been a nuisance; and discovered that I had a conscience.

My childhood memory of the teaching in Sunday School was less acute though I suppose I assimilated christian awareness as well as the next youngster. Probably a good yardstick would be that I gained knowledge and personal involvement from the hymns and I recollect one in particular which started: "I think, when I read that sweet story of old, when Jesus was here among men . . . and how he called little children to him" etc. The particular line I liked and which set me thinking was: "I wish that his hands had been placed on *my head*. . .", and later, when I was taught that "Jesus will come again", it led me to think deep thoughts which, even now, I would not care to divulge. Two disciplines affected and influenced me in my upbringing in the 'little chapel'; one was the regular attendance at Sunday School insisted upon by my parents and the system, and the other my voluntary acceptance of the discipline of the scout troop. An example concerning "the system" in the Sunday School was the weekly register of early and late attendances which determined the annual award of a 1st, 2nd or 3rd prize. There were no prizes for attendance only at the popular 2.30 pm session; to gain a first prize one had to register 104 early attendances in the 52 Sundays of the year by attending also the 10.00 am session which preceded the 11.00 am church service.

Our Sunday School secretary was very throrough and precise; a scholar's *"star card"* had to be in his hands promptly at 10.00 am and 2.30 pm. If he was carrying the reception basket toward his vestry as one came running in, he simply said: "You are late!" and you had to give your "star card" to your teacher and receive an 'O' stamp which was worth only half a mark. I think I gained only three or four *first* prizes during my ten years as a scholar and a few for $103^1/_2$ marks or less. The annual prize distribution was a great day to receive your book prize, containing a congratulatory label denoting the number of your attendances. A first prize was of value about two shillings (at the time, pre-1920, an adult labourer's wages was about thirty shillings).

Scouting was more voluntary and adventurous. Fortunately, for myself and the heroes who people my book, the scout troop was started from the Sunday School and led by men who were enthusiastic christians and able to attract scholars, several of whom became Sunday School teachers. Part of Robert Baden-Powell's genius, as he formed and developed Scouting, was the Patrol System. Grouping boys into gangs of about eight, who could compare with four or five similar patrols, enabled each boy to have a friendly and competetive identity. A patrol contained lads of 11 years and upwards one of whom, aged about fifteen perhaps, would be "leader" with maybe his younger friend as "second", and each of the others at a different stage of age and skill contributing to the prestige of the "Hawks, or "Beavers", or "Seagulls" (the latter being my choice).

To go camping with the scouts was not expensive for there was plenty of ex-army gear available at cheap prices; the army bell-tent at £3 could sleep about twenty boys and the cape-groundsheet (rubber on fabric) was two shillings per boy. With a demobbed soldier's back-pack and re-conditioned army blankets one felt very independent and capable. In the decade after the 1914-18 war we always relied on friendly farmers allowing us free camp sites. Later, maybe, I can tell my tale that I call *The Miracle of Forest Gate,* referring to a later period of 20 years free camp-ground, occurring in unusual circumstances.

Perhaps I should refer chiefly to *early* scouting times in which half of my book characters grew up. In the REV. DAN OAKES' missionary story I briefly told how he joined the scout troop from a day-school play centre and a further sentence or two had to suffice of his scout experience. But I scouted with him from his age of 13 to 21 and he was always interesting. He became the patrol leader of the OWLS and I led the GULLS. At the time scouting drew a lot of interest from primitive RED INDIAN life and we imitated their woodcraft lore, their tracking, signs, firelighting etc.

Making our camp-fire singsongs more romantic we made ourselves Indian costumes from hessian and each adopted a name which we solemnly used as we *pow-wowed.* Of course, I was *The Gull* and Dan, *The Owl.* He used to quote with heavy drama:

> "A wise old owl lived in an oak,
> The more he heard, the less he spoke;
> The less he spoke, the more he heard,
> I wish more people were like that bird!"

As we were each prone to come out with a camp-fire cry, with actions, it often happened that Dan would scream out:

> "Who'se the man with the big red nose?
> Oo-ah, oo-ah-ah!
> The man who laughs wherever he goes!
> Ooh-ah, Oo-ah-ah!"

But the practical training, things we read up in the Chief's book, Scouting for Boys, and his weekly pep-talk in *The Scout* boys' paper, along with badgework on many practical skills, certainly served Dan in good stead with his missionary work in wild island situations. Later, when he extravagantly took over as scoutmaster, together we once gatecrashed a Welsh scout camp situation to our advantage. A lord with a fine estate held an annual hospital fete on behalf of the Montgomeryshire hospitals, this was before the days of the N.H.S. He had invited troops of Welsh scouts to camp on his land and to perform steward duties at the great annual garden party fete during the week. We applied and duly turned up with about 25 of our scouts. We had a whale of a time and, in the course of our stewarding duties, Dan became a little involved with a clergyman who ran the book stall; He came away with many religious books. We fraternized well with the five Welsh troops and enjoyed camp-fires. The lovely countryside and swift-flowing River Severn, in which we swam, was a delight to our lads.

That was in the summer of 1926 and early in 1927 Dan responded to the urgent call of study for the Methodist Ministry in Australia and I became scoutmaster in his stead. I continued to take the troop to Montgomery until early in 1931 when I was spirited away by the L.M.S. Railway to their engine sheds at Stockport.

Both Dan Oakes and myself were greatly influenced by Fred Green (Chapter 9) and Syd Constable (Chapter 3) and I have briefly witnessed to that fact but I must now return to the Sunday School and Church scene, as I experienced it, and saw the effect on my various characters. At least two of my characters had a *conversion* experience at about the age of eleven. I certainly developed a belief and trust in Jesus as my Saviour, which is what *christian conversion* is supposed to be but I could not define a time and place as some christians can. I do remember testifying in a devotional meeting in the church parlour, when I was about sixteen, that I was thoroughly devoted to the Lord Jesus and I attributed it to experiences in the scout troop.

I remember it because an elderly official, who we took to be unfriendly to the scouts, said how pleased he was. Probably I was not completely correct for a dozen years of attending school, church, and its various activities undoubtedly led me to complete devotion long before that incident. However, I am sure that scouting was a catalyst, with its action and commitment, that enabled me to declare my conviction.

Elsewhere I have commended the Wesley Guild as a large group in the mid-week church activity because so many youths and girls were encouraged to do little things leading on to greater responsibility. I became the secretary of the Devotional Section and I had to lead my committee of about five to arrange a monthly evening of worship and activity. It was during that time that an important start was made with devotional plays, first started annually in the Guild, when Dan Oakes and I were principals in TOLSTOY'S plays, later developing into public performances on Good Fridays (in which I did *not* take part) which attracted a good audience from other churches. At the age of 18 I was invited by the Circuit Superintendent Minister to train as a Local Preacher as I had given one or two *papers* in the Guild. Dan Oakes was already preaching. I did not accept, giving two reasons: my railway job with steam engines and difficult turns of duty, and also the fact that I was practising the violin intensively. However I rated *action* above preaching, I think, at the time.

A couple of years earlier I had tried to teach in the Sunday School, it was a disaster. I had started to attend the Men's Bible Class, the final stage of the school. Most of the twenty-five members were teenagers up to the age of 20, plus a few older men; it was interesting, they discussed things. But just after they opened at 2.30 pm there would be a furtive knock at the door and a messenger from the junior or senior departments would beg one or more volunteers to fill a teacher vacancy. I felt a bit of compassion when a volunteer was not forthcoming and I was a bit proud of being a scout patrol leader. They let me try my prowess on a class of seven-year-olds; I was hopeless. Once more I tried with courage but incompetance. Weeks went by and then a teacher of 13-year-olds asked me to stand in for him one Sunday; I enjoyed it. Soon I was appointed as teacher to a dozen boys only about three years my junior.

We were having interesting times when the teacher of the senior class, a very nice middle-aged man who took boys in a room separate from the 150 who met in the church where I was, confessed that he had very difficult sessions — would I swop? I did, I enjoyed it, and ever after I stuck to the top class of boys.

In Chapter 9, I told of Fred Green re-organising the school on the newly popular graded lines, before I was twenty I was leader of the senior department (also teaching the senior class), responsible for ten classes with their teachers and the weekly preparation class.

Another call came to me in those years, less positive but quite real. A City Councillor was elected in our district; he was young and energetic and, because he also led a mens Bible class in the Church of England, he had been invited to speak in our church. It so happened that he later became a Member of Parliament, City Lord Mayor, etc., but on that early occasion he had said that christians should not feather-bed themselves *within* the church but take christian principles *out into life.* It caused me to gradually revise my attitude among workmates at the engine shed. The totally male workforce, serving under rather grim conditions, were certainly not polite company in language and habit. Quite rightly I had tried to observe christian standards aloof from the dominant crudity. Gradually, I am afraid very gradually, I accepted the mix of good and bad, and tried to be helpful as well as principled.

I joined the First Aid Team which was trained by members of St. John's and the local railway doctor. I looked more humbly at the better points of others whilst keeping to standards of language, thought and the *nones* of betting and drink. Sometimes I could put in a good word for those preferences. Like my father, I was a regular tradeunionist, but it was only as the years brought problems and revealed needs that the adventure of serving my fellow railwaymen opened out to a lifetime of interest. Many of these experiences I have dealt with in my book: "Life Adventure in Steam".

Whilst sketching a little of my adult life separate from the church, let me refer to two factors *after* my retirement from the railway in 1971. As I rode home on my bike on the last day, I called at the local home of the Leonard Cheshire Homes for Incurables: "Can I help in any way?", I asked, "Yes!", they replied and booked me to go in once a week. I served by feeding at table two or three patients who could not use their arms; made a few friends and sometimes pushed their wheelchairs on outings; this for $5^1/_2$ years.

Later, in 1982, after a lot of research, I started a club for unemployed young men with the help of a few other retired men from various local churches. We met for one afternoon per week in the church hall of the "little chapel" and continued for $6^1/_2$ years. A community officer was helpful and also the local police liaison officer; in fact the latter secretly recommended our club and the Merseyside Chief Constable awarded me a shield as "The Citizen of the Year for 1983", chosen from among his 23 police sections.

But I must return to the scout group for my younger friends of Chapters 5, 6, 7 and 8 were born after the year 1940. I have told you that my job took me away from Garston in 1931; to my sorrow our healthy scout troop, cub pack and Rovers barely lasted twelve months for they ceased to meet and the substantial equipment was scattered. In 1932 I married and our parents' homes remaining in Garston, we kept in touch with the "little chapel". At Edgeley Methodist Church, Stockport, we were afforded a welcome and friendships until we returned to Garston in 1937. Again I took an interest in their very large Sunday School and, in a necessarily limited way, their scout and youth groups. I rather fouled my reputation as I taught in the Sunday School for I spoke enthusiastically of modern methods in the *graded school* and, whilst the young responded happily, the *old brigade* were not impressed. I then saw a need on a new housing estate where a candidate for the Parliamentary Seat was meeting with children on Sunday afternoons in day school premises. I helped for about eighteen months before my job returned me to Garston. Taking rooms in Garston, close to the "little chapel", my wife and I were soon closely involved again. With my wife's sister I started a senior department of the school, meeting with 40 to 50 young teenage men and women in the chapel each Sunday afternoon. The venture was succeeding well as we came to the time of national emergency in 1938 when Prime Minister Chamberlain returned from Germany with his "peace in our time" agreement which was only the prelude to the war starting in 1939.

I was a keen pacifist but as our young men were approaching their eighteenth birthday and the compulsory call-up to H. M. Forces, I refrained from any influence that would complicate their position, particularly as I was in a reserved occupation and not subject to the call-up which very soon closed us down.

Nearly all our men under forty had to go and many of the women did various war service. In 1940 a German bomb blew out all the windows and devastated the roofs of the chapel and schoolrooms; for a time we met on Sundays in a Church of England building and weekday activities ceased.

Many stories could be told of those times; pehaps I can repeat one which had a humorous aspect. I was now living in a new house $2^1/_2$ miles from the chapel. A neighbour, who was a police inspector, drew my attention to a newspaper story that the local furniture factory had a large quantity of second-hand timber out in a field, and would welcome people to *take it away, free,* because of air-raid fire risk. We jumped at the offer, as new wood could not be bought, and loaded up our cycles, wheeled them, dangerously home. Suddenly I thought of our large schoolroom, which was bereft of windows and we were unable to use for meetings because of blackout restrictions. I hastened to the chapel and arranged for five men, with a large handcart, to attend the site before the crowds of opportunists had cleared the best timber. Excitedly, we loaded the cart to its maximum. Now the factory was managed by two brothers who were Jews. As we heaved our cart over rutted grassland, gaining speed as we reached the gateway, a man (he looked like a madman) sprang in front of us and almost run over before we could pull the cart to a halt. It was one of the Jewish brothers who was unaware of the action his brother had been forced to make.

Regardless of numerous other persons carrying motley loads of timber, he centred his passion on our well-loaded vehicle. I had to be the spokesman. He insisted that we turn back and unload, but *we* had a lot at stake. We did not sing to him: "We love the place, O Lord, wherein thine honour dwells", but later I thought it was extremely funny that I had begged and pursuaded a Jew to help us to make a Methodist church hall habitable again. I should have gone back to thank him after we had cobbled up our windows.

My return to the "chapel under-the-bridge" in 1937 had prompted some of the scouts I had left behind to press me to start the group again. It was impossible; my railway turns of duty revolved around a 24-hour day and seven-day weeks. In 1938 I took on a new house, an almost impossible financial burden for my wife and I with our two children. But two young men, ex-scouts, were very persistent; one was ARTHUR GOODALL, later to become the father of David, Keith and Colin of Chapters 5, 6 and 7. They said that if I would become "chief" again, they would run each parade night with any help that I could give.

I called a meeting of the Sunday school boys, 23 remained after school, and it was impossible for me to resist. The enthusiasm of ARTHUR and CHARLIE gave us quick success and we became re-registered as the "20th Allerton (Banks Road Methodist) Scout Group". Sydney Constable, whose Church of England scouts had been the 237th Liverpool whilst we had been the 135th Liverpool, now were ahead of us, bearing the title *16th* Allerton. Of course, Sydney's personal friendship and workmate relationship still persisted and on occasion he was very helpful to the new 20th.

I notice from my records that we started up in June 1940 with three patrols, Owl, Hawk and Wolf; in that Autumn our church hall H.Q. was devasted by the bomb so the reader will comprehend our wartime conditions that continued to 1945.

But still we made progress, started a cub pack, and until the middle years of the war we coped well; whilst I was firing steam engines around the country I was an enemy target along with my workmates. But soon I lost both my scout helpers on war service. Arthur Goodall served in India and did not see his baby son, David (who was to become a missionary doctor *in India*), until he was a toddler. He spent the later months of the war in Europe as a gunner on our South coast, shooting down "doodlebugs" (flying bombs) targetted devastatingly on London. When, in 1944, I was drafted to train jobs that lodged away from my home depot, the scout troop ignominiously closed.

But continuing as Sunday school superintendent I was constantly pressed to start the scouts again. My own two boys were coming to scout and cub age and I took them on a cycle-camping-hike. Arthur Goodall was out of the army now and I spent many months trying to persuade him to restart the troop under his leadership. Understandably, he and his wife had to repair the trauma of long-time separation. However, I had a trump card in my persuasive hand, little David was nearly eight years old, cub age. I was struggling along with a handful of boys of scout age when Arthur re-started. He would not accept the leadership but he started as cub Akela in September 1947 and so continued until 1949 when we were fortunate to accept the Allerton Scout Commissioner's wife as Akela and she was indeed a treasure until July 1970, over 20 years.

The cub pack was soon filled, chiefly with Sunday school boys, and in 1948 we were starting to promote boys into the troop. When Arthur became scoutmaster in 1949 things were starting to go very well, and in a further ten years his early cubs had not only established a troop to be proud of, but five of those boys had become warranted as Assistant Scoutmasters and it was during that period our "Over the Top" heroes of Chapters 5, 6, 7 and 8 blossomed forth. Additionally, one of those A.S.M.'s became a prominent and popular minister of the Presbyterian Church.

Of course, I did my stuff as Group S.M. in the organisational way and in practice at training and camps. We had good help from the Parents Committee and we formed a B.P. Guild of Old Scouts. I need not now dwell on very welcome successes, sufficient now to have sketched some of the circumstances and conditions that helped to mould the ten characters I admire so much. I do not even need to add, in the stories of their lives, how central JESUS was to them and, from my point of view, in all the history of our scout group and the church.

Through all our difficulties I treasure many occasions of what I call *heavenly coincidents,* where needs and solutions came together in unlikely circumstances. I am sure my present heroes all experienced such times as they ventured into the unknown. Such occasions, as in my Chapter 8, Harry Smith starts a quote: "With the enthusiasm of youth", and goes on to tell of his bold approach to the Billy Graham Evangelistic Association, offering to become Art Editor to their recently acquired *The Christian Newspaper* ("nearly a hundred years old and very dull" — according to Harry). His interviewer said: "We have just been advised by our MINIAPOLIS office to appoint a full-time Art Editor"; and gave young Harry the job. Or David Goodall, (Chapter 5), setting his heart on medical work in Africa and the opportunity to climb Mount KENYA! — suddenly being switched to a backward hospital in INDIA with remarkable results. In this context I can tell my little story of *The Miracle of Forest Gate.*

Re-starting the scout troop and pack after the war I felt a need to provide again the adventures of camping. I spent a full day cycling around the attractive area of DELAMERE FOREST in CHESHIRE , seeking a friendly farmer. I found none; after many miles and several calls. With mounting desparation I stopped near HATCHMERE LAKE to eat my sandwich and pray fervently. Still there was one possible farm, near to Hatchmere — an attractive bathing asset; I swung into the saddle with fresh zest. It was not to be, I left the farm for the long ride home, totally despondent.

As I regained the main road, slouching uphill, a voice came to me over the hawthorn hedge: "What's up mate?" It was a labourer in the field. I dismounted, glad of the sympathetic voice; he listened to my sad tale and gave me instant hope. "Turn left into that next lane and you will find a little farm; ask him, he'll help, I am courting his daughter!"

The farmer. MR POWELL, proved to be reticent and unlikely to agree to me bringing half-a-dozen little boys to camp in his field for a weekend. "I am only a tenant", he said, "The landowner would not allow it!" The bubble of my last hope had burst, but bravely (as they say) I continued in conversation, he seemed a kindly man. "As teenagers we used to camp on the fringe of the forest and swim in Hatchmere!", I told him, "And on Sundays we went to the tiny Methodist chapel". "Are you a Methodist?" he enquired. "Yes", I replied, "my lads are from the Sunday school". A smile enveloped his face and warmed my heart for he attended the tiny chapel. For twenty years, until his death, he welcomed our expanding number of boys on his fields and woods, coming with his wife each time to our "last night" camp fire. My angel in corduroys did marry his sweetheart and took over the responsibility of the Forest Gate farm when Mr Powell retired at 65, but still active. I purchased a fine walking stick as a retirement present from us all, with a silver band inscribed with our appreciation. After years of pleasure he arranged for the stick to lie with him in death.

In the New Testament, the last and most personal of the four gospels, St. John's, after sublime revelations of Jesus and his passion and resurrection, occurs a homely incident. A stranger on the shore, friendly to tired, dejected fishermen, had lit a fire and cooked bread and fish on the hot coals. He told them how to net more fish than they had ever dreamed of and in quiet companionship they ate a nourishing breakfast together. But his simple conversation with Peter, afterwards, was to nourish and haunt *mankind* for all time, as well as the big fisherman. Love was the theme, *ultimate love,* and the command, "Feed my sheep; take care of my lambs!" was the reason there was a little chapel under-the-bridge and the kind of people they turned out.

THE END

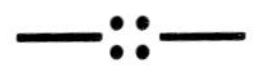

The Writer's Appreciation

As I re-read parts of Over The Top, I tremble a little and gasp to myself: "I could not have written that!"

Perhaps, also, at some point my characters similarly could conjecture: "I could not have done that!"

Is it undue presumption for me to refer to those pre-Ascension words of Jesus (recorded in ACTS:1,8), "But when the Holy Spirit comes upon you, you will be filled with power?" Shortly to leave his Apostles he certainly was speaking to *them,* but the subsequent history of the following 2,000 years does confirm that he also assures *us.*

So whilst I appreciate the help to me received from the characters you have been reading about, both recently and in the past; plus local people like the good lady of the typing, my own church minister, my family and the Liverpool District Chairman's encouragement — culminating in the sensitive Foreword that he has provided for this book, I can only summarize my appreciations in one word: 'Thankfulness!'

I hope that this book can fall into the hands of many blossoming children and young men and women who can see themselves as similar to these remarkable characters. Also that faithful folk in 'little chapels' and other fertile corners in our land may take heart and inspiration. That will indeed extend my Thankfulness.

Frank Mason.